KING ALFRED'S COLLEGE

Marketing
Mastering Your Small Business

Gloria Green
and
Jeffrey Williams

UPSTART
PUBLISHING COMPANY
Specializing in Small Business Publishing
a division of Dearborn Publishing Group, Inc.

This publication is designed to provide accurate and authoritative information in regard to the subject matter covered. It is sold with the understanding that the publisher is not engaged in rendering legal, accounting, or other professional service. If legal advice or other expert assistance is required, the services of a competent professional person should be sought.

Publisher and Acquisitions Editor: Jere L. Calmes
Editorial Assistant: Becky Rasmussen
Cover Design: Joni Doherty
Cover and Interior Illustration: Timothy Gibbons
Interior Design: Karen Billipp

Published by Upstart Publishing Company,
a division of Dearborn Publishing Group, Inc.

Printed in the United States of America
96 97 98 10 9 8 7 6 5 4 3 2 1

Authors: Gloria Green and Jeffrey Williams

Creative Writer: Mary G. Shuter

Produced under the direction of: Richard O. Schafer, Ph.D., Director, Distance Learning, Wisconsin Small Business Development Center, University of Wisconsin-Extension and Jeannette McDonald, DVM, Research Assistant

Content Advisors: Richard O. Schafer, John Mozingo, Sandy Lewandowski, and Fred Waedt

Contributions by: William H. Pinkovitz, Past Director; Erica McIntire, Director, Wisconsin Small Business Development Center, University of Wisconsin-Extension; Donald E. Hanna, Chancellor

Library of Congress Cataloging-in-Publication Data
Green, Gloria, 1955-
    Marketing : mastering your small business / Gloria Green and Jeffrey Williams.
        p.   cm.
    Includes bibliographical references (p.   ) and index.
    ISBN: 1-57410-020-3
    1. Marketing-- Planning. 2. Small business--Management.
    I. Williams, Jeff, 1948-   . II. Title.
    HF5415.122.G74 1996
    658.8--dc20   95-39461
                                                    CIP

Table of Contents

Preface

**Welcome to the
Business Mastery Certification Series**

*M*arketing: *Mastering Your Small Business* is one of five units from the **Business Mastery Certification Series**.

- **Marketing**
- Finance
- Human Resources
- Quality Management
- Legal Issues *or International (European) Business*

These materials have been designed to lead the learner through the process of mastering the business concepts necessary to a successful small business owner or manager. The structure of the materials; the Challenges and the Personal Workshops, coach the learner through the decision-making and growth process that is the basis for the mastery of these concepts. It is anticipated that the self-paced learner will take about 12 hours to complete the Challenges included in each unit. The flexibility of these materials also makes them a perfect instructional tool for use in classroom or distance education alternatives to independent study. If you are interested in the possible pursuit of either of these options, please contact the Business and Economics Section of the Independent Learning Program at the University of Wisconsin—Extension, at (608) 262-4876 or write to them at 432 North Lake Street, Room 201, Madison, WI 53706-1498 for more information.

The *Small Business Mastery Certificate* is awarded to the learner by the University of Wisconsin—Extension Department of Continuing Education upon satisfactory, accredited completion of the five courses in the Small Business Mastery series, signifying their proficiency in the management skills necessary to the successful small business owner or manager in the 21st century.

Your Challenge Begins

Successful small business marketing requires a shrewd combination of street-smart experience, access to reliable information, knowledge of the latest technology and gut instinct.

Virtually every activity your business undertakes influences your marketing—your business card design contributes or detracts from your image as a well-established company; how quickly you return phone calls reveals your overall professionalism; and how well you select your suppliers determines how well-thought-of your company is for on-time delivery.

You face the challenge of taking on larger competitors who can spend many times what you can to promote your business. You are often understaffed and overworked. So how do you keep your business moving ahead? By using the following ideas to make your marketing dollars go as far as possible:

• Analyze what you know already—customer buying patterns, competitors' pricing, etc., looking for "unclaimed sales dollars."

• Select one or two areas in which you feel you can deliver a superior product or service.

• Craft a selling message that zeroes in on how you will aid buyers and why they should buy from you.

• Experiment with different ways to communicate your sales message—compare return to investment, and stop if the ratio is unfavorable. Go on to the next idea.

• Review your plans regularly to assure that you are using a consistent message.

• Deliver customer service three times better than you yourself demand!

A sound marketing management system utilizes ongoing marketing research and organizes the results in a written marketing plan to assure a logical strategy and to provide goals and targets to be pursued. The marketing plan should be reviewed at least once per year to allow inclusion of new knowledge and techniques. Your promotional activities should be committed to a calendar and reviewed once per month to check your success in staying on schedule. And you should never stop learning!

To guide you in combining your marketing talents to create a coherent plan, this Marketing Management course is organized into four learning Challenges:

Challenge 1: Thinking Like A Customer

Challenge 2: Frugal Marketing Planning

Challenge 3: Crafting An Effective Marketing Mix

Challenge 4: Communicating With Your Market

Mastery Learning

This course has been designed for you to master marketing concepts outside the classroom. The Personal Workshops that you find in this guide encourage a different type of learning. You are no longer just reading a book. *You* will be actively involved in the learning process of what it takes to develop a sound marketing management system. Your mastery of these concepts will prove beneficial as you apply your newly acquired knowledge and skills to *your* business.

Marketing: Mastering Your Small Business is designed for you to apply your learning to your own business. This is your personal project. Enjoy!

What Are Personal Workshops?

Personal workshops are not tests, simply exercises and information-collecting forms designed to assist you in applying newly acquired techniques to your specific business.

Personal Workshops can be found throughout the Challenges. They are also located in the Personal Workshop section at the back of this guide.

You're Not Alone

Meet Jim, Marie, Jerry, and Nancy, owners of four small businesses all revolving around the same product—a line of Jamaican-style dips, salsas and sauces sold to specialty stores.

Jim manufactures the product line, Marie distributes it through her wholesaling company, Jerry owns a retail store that buys the product line from Marie, and Nancy runs an accounting service that handles the books for Jim, Marie and Jerry.

To guide you through the process of marketing planning, you will be joined by your new entrepreneurial friends, whose personal experiences with planning and executing marketing strategy will illustrate key points presented in your learning sessions.

Jim Copeland, Owner: Paradise Potions. As a long-time vacationer in the Caribbean islands, I was inspired by the memorable taste of the native sauces to create my own version of their tangy, fruit-based sauce which I initially prepared only for my friends. Encouraged by a neighborhood grocery store manager, I decided to try commercial production of my Lightning Jack sauce. I contracted with a local food packager to prepare the sauce according to my recipe, initially producing 500 jars. Imaginative use of taste testing (on a low budget) led to a rapidly spreading word-of-mouth promotional campaign, which resulted in several local restaurants requesting trials of both my seafood sauce and my salsa. Now, three years later, Paradise Potions annually ships 100,000 cases of uniquely flavored dips, salsas, and sauces to retail store and restaurant wholesalers and food brokers in a six-state territory.

Marie Nelson, Co-Owner: Le Caribe Wholesalers. I grew up in a family that treasured dinner time, because it gave my mother and father a chance to try out wonderful family recipes for our family. When I was ten years old, I promised myself that one day I would have my own business, bringing the foods that my mother and father loved so much to as many people as possible. Fresh out of high school, I went to work for an importer of ethnic foods from South America and the Caribbean. After having worked my way up from file clerk to warehouse manager, myself and three other key employees were given a chance to buy the business when the owner decided to retire. I became the new management group's marketing manager and chief new product developer. On one of my regular trips to a local ethnic food store featuring Caribbean products that month, I discovered Jim Copeland's Lightning Jack salsa and started a business relationship with Paradise Potions. This has resulted in Le Caribe becoming the lead distributor for their product line in its six-state selling territory.

Jerry Lee, Proprietor: Trade Winds Grocery. Even as a child I had a knack for making money with my ideas. I progressed from making donuts at home and selling them to local grocers to renting a vendor cart during summers in college to sell various handmade food delicacies. But my dream was to open my own small grocery store, specializing in sensational foods from Asia, South America and the Caribbean. Never afraid to try something new, I became known as "the place" to go when you wanted an unusual taste treat. I encouraged new food providers to put on taste testings in my store. It was at one of the early taste tests that I met Jim Copeland who had just started marketing the Lightning Jack sauce. A small initial order has led today to a monthly sales volume of over $4,000 of products from Paradise Potions. I introduced Jim Copeland to Marie Nelson.

Nancy Robinson, Accountant/Owner: Profit Plus Accounting Services. I studied accounting in college. My zeal for balancing accounts was somewhat tempered, however, when a summer internship at a large accounting firm in my home town turned out to be boring and unrewarding. I felt too limited in dealing with the client's accounting needs and vowed to go into my own accounting practice as soon as I could. Starting with a few clients on the side, while working in the accounting department of a large corporation, I finally took the plunge into my own business three years ago. One of my first full-time clients was Jim Copeland, who was struggling at the time to set up an effective inventory and accounts receivable system. My willingness to put in long hours and my proficiency in computerized accounting programs were well-suited to Jim's needs. Jim introduced me to Marie Nelson who in turn introduced me to Jerry Lee.

Learning Aids

The following icons are your learning aids. Highlighted in the margins of the page, these icons will provide you with study tips and valuable, interesting information on the topic of marketing management.

 For Your Information: Notes, quotes, and noteworthy information are located in an FYI box at the bottom of the page.

 Call Out: Information worth pointing out or remembering is called to your attention.

 Technology Tip: Advances in computer and telecommunications technology are already bringing rewards to the companies using them wisely. Useful applications are highlighted with this computer icon.

 Resource Tip: Others probably already know what you want to know. You will discover valuable resources where you see this resource book.

 Key Words/Phrases: Words and phrases that are considered business terms and are important to the understanding of the topic at hand are defined in the glossary.

 Step Back: Occasionally you will be asked to refer to an earlier step or workshop for purposes of review.

 Challenge Summary: At the end of each Challenge, you will find a summary of what you learned in the following four key areas. These designations are used throughout the four Challenges so you can systematically build on each technique.

 Information: This guide will provide you with pertinent business information as it relates to you on day-to-day matters as well as for strategic plans for your business.

Tools: Personal Workshops are the tools you will use to help you test and analyze your business ideas and strategies.

Learning: Running a business successfully involves you in ongoing learning. This learning will be selective and appropriate, fitting your business's needs and your skills, prior knowledge, experiences, and resources.

Networking: You will not be alone as you make your business decisions. You will be given access to additional outside resources to contact for support and assistance.

Self-Assessments

You are encouraged to complete the Self-Assessments that are located at the end of each Challenge. Self-Assessments are tools designed for you to check your understanding of the materials covered. If during your self-check, you find that you do not fully understand something, you will be directed to take another look at the material you have read. The guide will direct you to specific pages for review or to additional resources for help.

How to Read this Guide

Spend a few minutes previewing all of your materials before you begin. Become familiar with the guide and the accompanying Personal Workshops. Begin formulating questions in your mind that you want answered as you complete this guide.

Acknowledgments

Many thanks and a great deal of appreciation goes to Shelly A. McLaughlin at the University of Wisconsin SBDC. She labored tirelessly to give this book its "look" and freshness.

We would also like to extend our gratitude to Rosa A. Figueroa, Business Specialist at York College SBDC, Jamaica, New York; Greg Dobbins, Business Analyst and Jeanine Kowalski of Joliet Junior College SBDC in Joliet, Illinois for their advice and suggestions in helping us fine tune this book for the reader.

Challenge 1
Thinking Like A Customer

When you are running a small business, it is sometimes easy to become so overwhelmed by the breadth of details that you must personally handle that you lose focus on the most important asset for keeping your business going—the customer.

This Challenge is designed to allow you to take a breather, while you examine how you currently approach customer relationships. You will also look at some suggestions for creating even more productive connections to your customers.

If you are doing it successfully, marketing your business should be fun. It is, after all, the area of your business operations where you have the most regular chance to inject your personality. Marketing is the arena in which you prove that you really care about people. If your interest comes across as sincere, these same people will reward YOU beyond belief. Often they become your best salespeople.

But it takes a careful understanding of what you are really selling, who might want it and why they buy to succeed at small business marketing. It takes courage to pursue opportunities before their full potential is obvious. And most of all it demands a steadfast understanding of the following reality:

> *"In order to sell a product or a service, a company must establish a relationship with the customer. It must build trust and rapport. It must understand the customer's needs, and it must provide a product that delivers the promised benefits."*
>
> —Jay Conrad Levinson

> *"No opportunity is ever lost. If you fumble it, your competition will find it."*

Part One of this Challenge introduces you to the discipline of small business marketing. It introduces market-tested techniques for small business marketing that will help you to better compete in today's demanding business world.

Upon completion of Part One you will be able to:

- examine your current marketing from the point of view of your customers

- evaluate your marketing strengths and weaknesses

- assure that your business is "market driven" in its marketing conduct

- select your customers for maximum flexibility and profitability

- locate a special niche for your business

Part Two of this Challenge presents cost-effective techniques for conducting the market research you need to provide the facts and opinions essential to a useful marketing plan.

Upon completion of Part Two you will be able to:

- identify marketing problems for which you need additional information

- begin answering your questions with informal research

- design surveys, questionnaires and focus groups to derive direct information

- analyze and interpret your research findings to aid your marketing decision-making.

PART ONE:
Fundamentals of Small Business Marketing

Marketing for a small business is different from the marketing done by a large corporation. What are the differences?

Small businesses have to attract and sell to customers using the least amount of money they can to get the job done. They cannot afford expensive mistakes, so they experiment all the time—with their pricing, their sales approach, their sales promotion pieces, etc. The key is to research, formulate some action steps, try them for a month or so and then evaluate the results. If you are not getting the expected results, try something else. You realize quickly that you cannot afford to throw money at potential customers!

Many small business owners do not consider themselves as natural salespeople. Sometimes the thought of selling makes them very nervous. What many business owners want is for customers to magically appear so that they can spend most of their time producing their product or service to supply them. Much of the fear in running a business comes from worrying that you won't ever have enough customers to allow you to stay in business.

If you feel that you are not a natural talent when it comes to selling, remember:

> *"I am the world's worst salesman: therefore I must make it easy for people to buy."*
>
> —F. W. Woolworth

Marketing is a collection of methods that you use to keep the customers coming without having to be the world's greatest salesperson. Successful marketing allows you more time to produce and create new products because it requires less time to prospect for customers.

What Are the Best Methods?

Effective marketing makes people want to buy your product or service. How you achieve this depends upon several factors:

- **Your type of business.** For example, much of the marketing for retailers has do with their location.

- **Your personality**. If, for example, you like to laugh, you can use appropriate humor in your marketing (but be careful).

- **Your money**. What is your marketing budget? Almost every marketing idea comes with a price tag. For example, direct mail marketing can easily run over $1.00 per piece to design, print and mail.

- **Your time**. For example, if you have someone make your product for you on contract, it will leave you more time for marketing.

In order for a small business to sell a product or service, it must establish a relationship with its customers. It must build a reputation for trust. Above all else, it must understand and do everything possible to meet the customers' needs.

 Paradise Potions, Jim Copeland: What we want our customers to remember most is: (1) All-natural ingredients; (2) Shipping cartons can be easily converted into endcap displays; (3) We back product up with an aggressive sampling program.

 Le Caribe Wholesalers, Marie Nelson: The three key features of our business that we want to plant in our customers' minds are: (1) Computerized order picking assures quick shipment; (2) On-going development of in-store promotions for our products; (3) Active cooperation with manufacturers in developing new variations of products and new product segments.

 Trade Winds Grocery, Jerry Lee: We would like our customers to most remember the following aspects of our marketing: (1) Special order desk promptly searches for requested products that we do not now carry and we try to get a sample for the customer; (2) We feature in-store cooking and preparation classes each weekend to illustrate how to use many of our more exotic products; (3) "No-waiting" checkout.

 Profit Plus Accounting Services, Nancy Robinson: The three major marketing messages we would like to get across to our clients are: (1) We are a "one-stop" source of accounting services—everything from software installation to bank lending packages; (2) We are well-versed in all small business accounting software and offer set-up package at fixed price; (3) We are backed up by CPAs specializing in taxes, retail operations and bank borrowing.

Ask yourself: "What unmet need does my product or service satisfy?" Once you have answered this question, you have determined the core of your marketing strategy. All you have left to do is persuasively communicate the benefits of your product or service to the customer and deliver those benefits on time.

 FYI

Personal Workshop Preparation #1: Thinking Like the Customer

The first step in creating a relationship with your customers is to think like they do. Pretend you are in their position and you are approached by someone selling your product. What would you want to know? What assurances would you want? How would you establish credibility and a feeling of reliability? What benefits would you expect?

You will have an opportunity in Personal Workshop #1 to evaluate how accurately you have listened to and observed your customers' needs. Before you begin the workshop, however, examine how case study entrepreneur Jim Copeland completed this first workshop.

THE PURPOSE OF THIS WORKSHOP IS TO EXAMINE YOUR CURRENT MARKETING POLICIES FROM THE CUSTOMER'S POINT OF VIEW.

Personal Workshop #1

Thinking Like the Customer

Imagine that you are the customer and that you are skeptical about parting with your money for the product or service your company offers. Determine from your answers how well you convince yourself that your company satisfies your needs.

1. What are the three most important things you want me to know about your product or service?

#1: All natural ingredients

#2: Shipping cartons easily converted into displayers

#3: Our products are backed up with an aggressive sampling program

2. Why are they important to me?

#1: Approximately 10% of the retail food market is now made up of "green consumers," dedicated to environmentally safe products and products that are safe to their bodies. These people spend, on average, 22% more each month for food than typical consumers.

#2: Many of our accounts are small specialty food stores with limited space and staff. Our shipping containers are designed to easily convert into eye-catching, end-of-aisle display units, thus presenting a professional appearance at no additional expense and saving the store employees time.

#3: Food retailers know that new food items must be tasted to attract real users. We make tasting our products fun with imaginative in-store promotions built around tasting the product, learning how to cook with it, or how to use it as a flavorful accent.

3. How does your product/service excel when compared with others?

#1: We go beyond taste with our product development. We carefully consider the consumer's total lifestyle—dietary desires, time restraints, and social activities—when we create our new recipes.

#2: We often become unpaid promotional consultants to our smaller accounts, aiding them in developing imaginative tie-ins between our products and related products.

#3: We are scientific in making sure our product assortment uses store space efficiently. We will run a computer-generated shelf plan for your store.

4. How do you feel your company is better and different from my current supplier?

We are very good at finding the ongoing interest people have in what may appear to be trendy food items. We find the basic tastes and textures they want again and again. We help them learn how to easily incorporate our products into their existing diet.

5. Why should I believe that you know what you are doing?

We have won the Natural Food Association's "New Taste" award three years in a row.

6. How do you make it more convenient for me to buy than does my current supplier?

Our salespeople are equipped with lap-top computers and built-in modems that allow them to continually show our on-hand position and to fax in your orders right from the store. We provide an expected ship date before they leave.

7. How does your pricing compare with my current supplier?

Our pricing is comparable to pricing on the premier versions of similar product lines. And we provide faster turn-around time, thus reducing your annual inventory costs and increasing your bottom line.

THE PURPOSE OF THIS WORKSHOP IS TO EXAMINE YOUR CURRENT MARKETING POLICIES FROM THE CUSTOMER'S POINT OF VIEW.

Personal Workshop #1
Thinking Like the Customer

Imagine that you are the customer and that you are skeptical about parting with your money for the product or service your company offers. Determine from your answers how well you convince yourself that your company satisfies your needs.

1. What are the three most important things you want me to know about your product or service?

> #1:

> #2:

> #3:

2. Why are they important to me?

> #1:

> #2:

> #3:

3. How does your product/service excel when compared with others offering it?

> #1:

> #2:

> #3:

4. How do you feel your company is better and different from my current supplier?

5. Why should I believe that you know what you are doing?

6. How do you make it more convenient for me to buy than does my current supplier?

7. How does your pricing compare with my current supplier?

Workshop Follow-Up

 1. Recheck what you think your marketing communications are saying to existing and prospective customers. You may be surprised by a mismatch of what they want to hear and what your marketing says to them.

 2. Examine how you establish credibility with potential customers.

 3. Evaluate how well you have kept up with new competition in making purchase of your product or service convenient.

What Makes Effective Marketing

It is sometimes mistakenly thought that you perform marketing only until you find some customers. Then you switch into production. People who develop this attitude toward marketing tend to make use of promotion and advertising only when times are tough. In fact, the most rapidly growing corporations in America rely on continuous marketing campaigns, in good times and bad.

Before you begin to explore specific ways you can attract customers, you need to understand what marketing experts tell us about the process:

> *"The only truly essential element for a successful business is having enough people buy your product or service, week after week, month after month, year after year."*
>
> —Paul and Sara Edwards

- Marketing is an investment, not an expense.
- It must be done continually.
- It must communicate a consistent message.
- It should show your passion for your business.

Admittedly, when you write the check for a $900 newspaper ad, marketing sure seems like an expense, but it is truly an investment in the future of your company. Like any investment, it may end up being a loss of money or a profitable return. Patience has a lot to do with achieving a positive result.

Too many small businesses only pump up their promotional spending when sales slow down. Why do you think sales slowed down? Perhaps the business stopped trying to find new customers whose needs it could potentially satisfy. Or maybe the business stopped telling its current customers how valuable they were. Finding and keeping customers is the essence of successful marketing.

Without a marketing strategy, your company heads out with no clear end result in sight. If you do not know what you wish to achieve, it is very likely you also don't know what to say to potential customers to persuade them to help you achieve your goal. Knowing what you want to achieve makes it much easier to communicate consistently because you understand well what reaction you wish from your customers.

Selling experts will tell you that one trait more than any other determines how successful you are in selling: the enthusiasm in your presentation. Sincere enthusiasm can only come from truly enjoying what you do and sincerely believing that you offer an improvement over what is already available.

It is useful at this point to examine your current approach to marketing. How dedicated are you to regularly communicating a consistent message? Are you willing to invest in your marketing?

Paradise Potions, Jim Copeland: We have tried to keep our promotional expenditures around 10 percent of our projected sales each year for the past three years. This has meant tight cash flow at times but it has resulted in a steady stream of new prospects among specialty food outlets. The key message we want to leave with every prospect we contact is: we supply all-natural products at prices competitive with grocery store brands, backed by a constant search for better ways to sell our products.

Le Caribe Wholesalers, Marie Nelson: We use co-operative advertising with our manufacturers whenever possible to expand our promotional dollars. We have become known for concocting imaginative joint promotions involving several manufacturers at the same time. Since many of our suppliers are small to medium-sized manufacturers, we are almost an extended marketing department to them.

Trade Winds Grocery, Jerry Lee: Our reputation has been built on being the first to try new ethnic food items and back them with aggressive in-store taste-testing, cooking demonstrations and take-home recipes. This costs us extra money to pay an outside writer and illustrator, but it has paid off in sales growth. We want our customers—largely young professionals—to feel that a visit to our store is entertaining.

Profit Plus Accounting Services, Nancy Robinson: I deal with smaller clients who often feel that they will have to sacrifice marketing funds to pay an accountant on a monthly basis. By properly installing their accounting software and showing them what they can do each month, I reduce my expense to them while providing them with a highly usable expense control system.

Personal Workshop Preparation #2: How We Market Now

Personal Workshop #2 provides you with the opportunity to examine your current approach to marketing and to determine where you may not be following the four keys to successful marketing.

In preparation of Personal Workshop #2, examine how case study entrepreneur Marie Nelson completed this next exercise.

THE PURPOSE OF THIS WORKSHOP IS TO EVALUATE HOW MUCH TIME AND MONEY YOU ARE NOW INVESTING IN YOUR MARKETING; TO DETERMINE WHAT YOUR MESSAGE IS; AND WHAT STEPS YOU TAKE TO BE CONSISTENT IN COMMUNICATING YOUR MESSAGE.

Personal Workshop #2
How We Market Now

1. In the past year, how many dollars did you invest in marketing?

$ 25,000

2. For comparison, how many dollars did you spend in the past year on your business vehicle?

$ 12,000

3. List below, by month, any major market research or promotional activity you completed in the past year:

January: New product survey—suppliers

February: New product "showcase" tour of retailers

March: Promotional planning visits to key retail accounts. In-store calendar

April: In-store demonstrations

May: In-store demonstrations

June: Local trade show demonstrations; Chamber expo presentations

July: Fall promo meetings with retailers. Season end reviews with manufacturers.

August: Vacation break

September: New product survey—suppliers

October: In-store demos

November: In-store demos; seasonal promotions

December: Seasonal promotions and gift marketing

4. I am a stranger and I ask you what your marketing message is. What would you say?

We go beyond simply distributing and promoting ethnic and gourmet food products. We actively assist manufacturers in new product development and retailers in new promotion development.

5. Do you approach your sales promotion literature with a single theme?

Yes (x)   No ( )

6. If Yes, what is your theme?

We provide monthly, new product orientations, involve all of our employees in our in-store demonstrations and provide low-cost catering for employee events to provide on-going taste test focus groups.

7. Do you utilize consistent design, color, paper, etc. to tie together your materials?

Yes (x)   No ( )

8. Are all employees trained to give the same, basic marketing story about your business?

Yes (x)   No ( )

THE PURPOSE OF THIS WORKSHOP IS TO EVALUATE HOW MUCH TIME AND MONEY YOU ARE NOW INVESTING IN YOUR MARKETING; TO DETERMINE WHAT YOUR MESSAGE IS; AND WHAT STEPS YOU TAKE TO BE CONSISTENT IN COMMUNICATING YOUR MESSAGE.

Personal Workshop #2
How We Market Now

1. In the past year, how many dollars did you invest in marketing?

$

2. For comparison, how many dollars did you spend in the past year on your business vehicle?

$

3. List below, by month, any major market research or promotional activity you completed in the past year:

January

February

March

April

May

June

July

August

September

October

November

December

4. I am a stranger and I ask you what your marketing message is. What would you say?

5. Do you approach your sales promotion literature with a single theme?

   Yes ( )   No ( )

6. If Yes, what is your theme?

7. Do you utilize consistent design, color, paper, etc. to tie together your materials?

   Yes ( )   No ( )

8. Are all employees trained to give the same, basic marketing story about your business?

   Yes ( )   No ( )

Workshop Follow-Up

 1. Assess whether your investment level in marketing is keeping you in contact with customers as often as you desire.

 2. Reexamine how well your sales promotion materials fit together. Do they provide a smooth, coordinated look and story?

 3. Look at how well you work within a marketing events calendar. Are you realistic in the length of time needed to bring a new marketing campaign to the market?

 4. Evaluate how well each employee contributes to accurate and compelling marketing communications. Is more training required?

Being Market Driven

Starting with the end of World War II until the late 1970s, many of America's major corporations decided what to manufacture based largely on what made their machines run most efficiently. They were production-oriented whether it was the most convenient option for the customer or not. For example, do you remember when you could only do your banking from 10 o'clock until 3 o'clock? Scheduling personnel was more important to banks than satisfying customers.

> *"We follow the law of demand and supply."*
>
> —Anonymous

A new generation of smart, knowledgeable and demanding customers has been developing since the late 1970s. They don't really care what your production problems are, they want service. They want you to ask them regularly what they need and want. And they would like to feel that they had some input in the final product or service. Smart marketers have picked up on this dramatic change in customer mentality and expectations and have noticeably modified the way they go about developing new products and services.

When you first ask customers what they want and then make a product or service to satisfy their wants, you are exhibiting a marketing strategy known as being "market driven." Even banks have caught on to this change. Consider the banking innovations over the past ten years. Automatic tellers. Weekend hours. Branch banks all over town. Phone services. Interest bearing checking accounts. Bank deregulation led to increased competition, which in turn has resulted in a much more pronounced pro-customer attitude.

Trade Winds Grocery, Jerry Lee: Food retailing may represent the essence of being a market-driven company. We create none of the products we sell ourselves; we are just the conduit between the food manufacturer and the food consumer. Since food is such an intensely personal consumption, people's attitude toward any particular food can change unexpectedly as their outlook on life changes. Food is a reward as well as sustenance. People like to receive entertainment along with their food. In our store we work hard to combine useful health information with variety and a sense of entertainment through our food tastings, cooking classes and expert demonstrations. We see our challenge as creating a food buying experience that results in a lift for the consumer, not a headache. To do this effectively, we frequently survey our consumers—through direct mail, in-store questionnaires, reviews of demonstrations, and very importantly, by reading the contents of our suggestion box.

Profit Plus Accounting Services, Nancy Robinson: Most business people don't associate accountants with any customer-responsive marketing techniques—we are often looked at as a necessary evil. Our popularity ranks right up there with the dentist. I have worked hard since starting my business to come across as knowledgeable of the tax laws while still appearing as the entrepreneur I have always considered myself. I show my clients that I think about their business in the same market-driven way they do, but I add discipline to the process by regularly prompting my clients to take financial stock—to honestly evaluate how profitable their activities are. I don't want my clients to feel they have to "ask my permission," but instead I want them to include me in their deliberations at an early stage as a valuable source of information and as a sounding board.

Personal Workshop Preparation #3: Is Your Business Market Driven?

If you are not running your company on a market driven basis, it is very likely that your competitors are. Examine what you are doing today. Personal Workshop #3 examines how well you take into consideration your customers' needs and wants before you embark on introducing new products or services.

In preparation for Personal Workshop #3, examine how case study entrepreneur Jim Copeland completed this exercise:

THE PURPOSE OF THIS WORKSHOP IS TO FOCUS MORE EFFECTIVELY ON WHAT YOU CAN DO TO IDENTIFY CUSTOMER NEEDS AND RESPOND MORE SUCCESSFULLY TO THEM.

Personal Workshop #3
Is Your Business Market Driven?

1. Do you conduct research on customer needs before you design a new product or service?

   Yes (X)   No ( )

1a. If No, why not?

2. Can you directly relate your product or service features to documented customer needs?

   Yes(X)   No( ) If Yes, pick one product for Questions 2a-2c.

2a. Which product/service?

   Lightning Jack Jamaican Sauce

2b. Which feature?

   Two versions: mildly spicy, and "zingy"

2c. Which need?

   Consumer research revealed that the same consumer wished a milder version for serving to guests and a tangier version for their personal use.

3. How often do you survey the satisfaction of your customers?

   For our supplier-customers, at least once per quarter; for our retail accounts, twice per year on major promotional planning. On every delivery for day to day marketing problems.

3a. How do you do this?

   Through formal semi-annual meetings and informal in-store conversations between our distribution staff and our customers.

4. Do you routinely ask for customer suggestions?

   Yes (X)   No ( )

5. If Yes, how do you do this?

   Several ways: Phone checks with store managers; face to face interaction between our delivery people and the store stocking staff. These people often spot problems and opportunities much earlier than the store manager.

6. Do you maintain detailed records on customer background, needs, past comments?

   Yes (X)   No (   )

7. Do you train all employees in selling new products or service?

   Yes (X)   No (   )

8. Have you given your employees a written policy on handling customer complaints and requests for return?

   Yes (X)   No (   )

9. If Yes, do you use customer complaints to improve your product or service?

   Yes (X)   No (   )

THE PURPOSE OF THIS WORKSHOP IS TO FOCUS MORE EFFECTIVELY ON WHAT YOU CAN DO TO IDENTIFY CUSTOMER NEEDS AND RESPOND MORE SUCCESSFULLY TO THEM.

Personal Workshop #3
Is Your Business Market Driven?

1. Do you conduct research on customer needs before you design a new product or service?

   Yes (   )   No (   )

1a. If No, why not?

2. Can you directly relate your product or service features to documented customer needs?

   Yes (   )   No (   ) If Yes, pick one product for Questions 2a-2c.

2a. Which product/service?

2b. Which feature?

2c. Which need?

3. How often do you survey the satisfaction of your customers?

3a. How do you do this?

4. Do you routinely ask for customer suggestions?

Yes ( ) No ( )

5. If Yes, how do you do this?

6. Do you maintain detailed records on customer background, needs, past comments?

Yes ( ) No ( )

7. Do you train all employees in selling new products or services?

Yes ( ) No ( )

8. Have you given your employees a written policy on handling customer complaints and requests for return?

Yes ( ) No ( )

9. If Yes, do you use customer complaints to improve your product or service?

Yes ( ) No ( )

Workshop Follow-Up

 1. Acknowledge if you perform market research regularly. If so, how do you organize it to achieve the most beneficial result?

 2. Examine how well you encourage your customers to talk to you—and how well you listen. For example, can you identify one substantial selling success in the past year that arose from receiving specific information from your customers?

 3. Evaluate how well you make your customers feel appreciated.

Selecting Your Customers

Many people become self-employed to gain the sense of freedom that comes from being your own boss. It is often true that you do gain a greater sense of control over your life when you go out on your own. But never mistake the essence of successful business: your customers become your bosses. Your objective is to win their trust and thereby enjoy their help.

There are only two ways to get money for your business: borrow it or generate it from customer sales. Unless you have very "deep pockets" you will most likely prefer the second option—sales.

Effective marketing centers around finding the unmet customer need and focusing like a laser beam on satisfying it everyday, no matter what other problems you are facing. It comes down to keeping your boss(es) happy!

However, you must exercise some caution as you plan your marketing strategy to satisfy these needs. Every marketing activity comes with a cost, and sometimes the cost is just too high relative to the selling price to make it attractive enough to carry out.

It takes trial and error to learn how to balance customer satisfaction and profitability. No one formula works all the time. Blended in together are sales where you cut your profit to the minimum, sales where you hit the jackpot and sales that are about average. Flexibility is the key to successful small business marketing—don't set your policies in concrete!

> *"I was successful because you believed in me."*
>
> —Ulysses S. Grant

One of the most attractive features of being a small business owner or manager is that to a large extent you can choose your customers, thereby choosing your boss. Your marketing strategy determines to a great extent which customers you end up with. You have the power to create a strategy that will result in the type of customers you wish. Of course, some types of businesses tend to be known for a rough and tumble style of operating, such as selling steel or chemicals or collecting past-due debts. You are expected to be tough in these industries, so be forewarned!

Many business owners focus only on the ability of customers to generate cash. There are other important benefits you can receive from your customers, if you look for them.

Included among these are new knowledge, a chance to make mistakes trying new techniques, and an opportunity to access business social settings you cannot enter on your own. Take some time to reexamine your current customer base to determine the full extent of the benefits they can offer you. Ask yourself: Are we taking advantage of all that we can?

FYI

There are three types of customers you need:

1. Those who help you even out your income flow
2. Those who help you upgrade your skills
3. Those who help you respond to business changes

What Does This Mean for Your Business?

You would to like to think that every customer will be a regular repeat customer. But the truth is that due to a lot of factors inside of your customer's business, the ordering pattern may be highly unpredictable. For some customers you can never seem to do enough. Others are very rigid in their time schedules, even when they cause the delay.

Key Word

What you should be looking for as the core of your sales are a group of customers with a predictable buying pattern, who appreciate what you do for them (and tell others) and who are willing to give a little bit in those rare cases where you find yourself with too much work at one time. These customers make up your target market, and will most benefit from your service **niche** or product. You will only find these customers if you make a plan to look for them.

Three Types of Customers

One of the key reasons that small business is very successful in competing with much larger companies is that small business owners are often the first to embrace new skills and technology. Examples include alpha-numeric pagers, laptop computers, mail box stores, etc. No matter how "tuned in" you think you are, you cannot be everywhere at one time. Your customers can help you keep up-to-date.

Two types of clients can make a big difference in keeping you informed: those who challenge you and those who allow you to learn on the job. Don't shy away from the customers who challenge you and whose demands will require knowledge you don't have right now. You can get it. Life is a lot more enjoyable if you stretch mentally on a regular basis.

Also consider the clients who allow you the opportunity to learn as continuing education. These clients often want to learn as you do through your communication with them. They will lead you to sources of information on new developments within your industry, such as specialty trade shows, newsletters, trade magazines, and trade association reports.

The third class of customers we seek are those who are leaders in their industries—who others turn to when they need information. To achieve these relationships, you need to have a customer base that is as broad and diversified as possible. Having a diverse base means catering to a wide range of customer needs. For example, a computer consultant who sells an "off the shelf" software product, customizes it, recommends equipment and system changes, and connects equipment can satisfy the needs that a variety of end-users might have. Some of the people you want to stay in touch with you may know through non-business activities such as the youth baseball league. Others you may know from volunteer work. But be careful: Serving a diverse customer base can lead you away from your focus on one central business concept.

A healthy business needs all three types of customers, but keeping them all happy requires a flexible strategy on profitability. For example, you might provide consulting to a particular customer for no charge because you believe that the outcome can be used with others as an example of your competency.

Customer Awareness

A customer-selection approach to marketing requires that each and every employee of your business has an awareness of who your top customers are, something about what they buy and the ability to answer basic questions or to know who to refer them to for an answer. In a small business, there cannot be any such luxury as an employee who "just answers the phone."

For instance, a small accounting firm in southern Wisconsin hires an office manager to help with day-to-day operations. Among her responsibilities is "marketing," which until now has consisted of preparing brochures and advertisements for the yellow pages and local newspaper.

During her first week on the job, the office manager notices that the company's secretary does not answer the phone promptly. When the secretary does answer the phone, her manner is often curt, as if she considers the call an interruption. The overworked secretary also handles billing, but because she has so many other tasks, billing mistakes are common. The bills go out on small forms, written in some sort of code that only the secretary seems to understand. Customers complain that they can't read or understand their bills.

What do these problems have to do with the accounting firm's marketing program? Everything! Beautiful brochures prepared by the office manager may win attention of potential clients, but those prospects are likely to be turned off by their first phone call to the firm—or their cryptic bill.

What you don't do can influence which customers you select as much as what you do.

 Paradise Potions, Jim Copeland: It has been a real challenge to maintain a balance of customers. Since it is almost impossible to get our products on the shelves of major grocery store chains, we must target independent grocers, specialty food shops, restaurants, mail order and employee incentive programs. Sometimes, if one customer in a category in a given city is doing business with us, his or her competitors will refuse to do business with us. It is a constant struggle to show that we are so outstanding in our service that no store can do without our product line.

 Le Caribe Wholesalers, Marie Nelson: When we started in food distribution, we had to take the suppliers we could get. That hurt our reputation in some cases. Now we balance profitability, visibility, reliability and reputation when approaching new potential suppliers.

Trade Winds Grocery, Jerry Lee: My location is critical to my customer mix. Although I pay more for rent than I would like, our close proximity to a major private university provides us with a diverse group of customers. They, however, are well-educated and as a result are very demanding. If we are out of stock on their favorite snack food just once, they threaten to go elsewhere. Fortunately for our profit margins, these people are also major impulse buyers—usually products that carry higher profit margins for us.

Profit Plus Accounting Services, Nancy Robinson: It is difficult sometimes to convince a five- to six-year old company that they are lacking something in their accounting system. Since most owners are not well-educated in accounting, they tend to diminish the process to a monthly profit and loss statement, with little understanding of how to use financial statements to manage for better profits. I have been able to get my foot in the door with a number of new accounts by showing them first how to save money on one major expense. Despite the assistance I provide, it is difficult to get them to pay me a reasonable fee. I have to balance tax return clients, software clients, and consultation clients to produce the profit I desire.

Personal Workshop Preparation #4: Our Current Customer Family

Personal Workshop #4 explores what mix of customers your business enjoys today.

In preparation for Personal Workshop #4, examine how case study entrepreneur Nancy Robinson completed this workshop.

THE PURPOSE OF THIS WORKSHOP IS TO FOCUS ON HOW WELL YOU CURRENTLY MIX THE THREE TYPES OF CUSTOMERS PRESENTED ABOVE. IT PROVIDES GUIDANCE IN ADJUSTING YOUR MARKETING EFFORTS TO BETTER ACHIEVE THE BALANCE BETWEEN CUSTOMER SATISFACTION AND PROFITABILITY.

Personal Workshop #4
Our Current Customer Family

1. What percentage of your customers account for 80% of your sales?

30%

1a. List the names of your key customers (or attach a computer printout):

Paradise Potions   FoodWorks
Trade Winds Grocery   SeaBreeze Creations
Le Caribe Wholesalers   HyperComp Distributors

2. On average, how many times did the typical customer in this group buy from you last year?

> *4 times per year, generally once per quarter*

3. How could you go about getting just one more order per year from each of them?

> *Add new consulting services such as installing inventory control software.*

4. What new skills, techniques or technology did you learn about in the past year from your customers?

> *Using electronic media to promote to and communicate with customers.*

5. Which specific customers provided this new knowledge?

> *Paradise Potions and Le Caribe Wholesalers*

6. How do you go about finding the "knowledge rich" customer?

> *By being an informed consumer—we often find the most advanced clients through purchases we make for our customers.*

7. When you want to know the latest in your business, which customers do you call?

> *Le Caribe Wholesalers for computer technology, FoodWorks for new promotional mechanisms.*

8. What methods for staying in touch with business leaders do you find most convenient (personal contact, newsletters, on-line, etc.)?

> *Personal contacts and newsletters targeted to their specific interests in new techniques.*

9. What communication methods have you been wanting to try?

> *The Internet.*

THE PURPOSE OF THIS WORKSHOP IS TO FOCUS ON HOW WELL YOU CURRENTLY MIX THE THREE TYPES OF CUSTOMERS PRESENTED ABOVE. IT PROVIDES GUIDANCE IN ADJUSTING YOUR MARKETING EFFORTS TO BETTER ACHIEVE THE BALANCE BETWEEN CUSTOMER SATISFACTION AND PROFITABILITY.

Personal Workshop #4
Our Current Customer Family

1. What percentage of your customers account for 80% of your sales?

_____%

1a. List the names of your key customers (or attach a computer printout):

2. On average, how many times did the typical customer in this group buy from you last year?

3. How could you go about getting just one more order per year from each of them?

4. What new skills, techniques or technology did you learn about in the past year from your customers?

5. Which specific customers provided this new knowledge?

6. How do you go about finding the "knowledge rich" customer?

7. When you want to know the latest in your business, which customers do you call?

8. What methods for staying in touch with business leaders do you find most convenient (personal contact, newsletters, on-line, etc.)?

9. What communication methods have you been wanting to try?

Workshop Follow-Up

 1. Examine which customers really keep your business going. Are you appreciative of them? Do you involve them in recommending new customers?

 2. Can you highlight one sales success in the past year that resulted from new knowledge provided by a customer? If no, think about how you can better access market information from your customers.

 3. Review new methods of marketing communication you have not tried but would like to try.

The "guru" of the small business marketing movement is the author of the best-selling "Guerrilla Marketing" series. The volume that presents a comprehensive presentation of marketing tactics for small business is *The Guerrilla Marketing Handbook,* by Jay Conrad Levinson, Boston: Houghton-Mifflin & Co., 1994, ISBN 0-395-70013-2.

 FYI

PART TWO:
Do-It-Yourself Market Research

Once you have diagnosed the current condition of your company's marketing you may realize that you would benefit from additional information.

> *"It's the oldest lesson in the world: unless you're customer-driven, you go out of business."*
>
> —Walter Wriston

Marketing research is the process of gathering information about your target market(s). As simple as that may sound, some people have misconceptions about this process because of the many forms it can take.

Market research is a planned and organized effort to gather facts to help make better business decisions. It can be a complex, costly and time-consuming venture, but more often it is simple and straightforward. Market research need not involve thousands of surveys and sophisticated statistics to provide the answers you need to solve business problems quickly and inexpensively. For example, if you regularly read the newspaper ads of competing businesses, you're researching the market. See how quick and easy it can be?

Why Research?

The first step in conducting market research is to figure out what you want to learn. Get specific. What do you hope to accomplish through your research effort? What do you need to know, and why?

An easy way to assess the need for market research is to put things down on paper:

• What's the problem?

• Does it involve product selection, customer service, training, location, advertising or another issue?

• What are the possible solutions?

• What information do you need to decide? Will customer attitudes help you choose an option? Do you need information on competitors?

After you've sorted out the problem, the potential solutions and the information you need to decide, you can begin market research.

Paradise Potions, Jim Copeland: One of my most pressing unsolved marketing problems right now is how to get our products into the premium and incentive marketplace. Special packaging demanded by the large corporations could set us back a pretty penny. I cannot afford to take that risk until I learn more about the ordering patterns in the industry, the average profit margins, the sales promotion material requirements, as well as other key information.

Trade Winds Grocery, Jerry Lee: My store's profit margins are being squeezed by the new type of "natural food" grocery store starting to spread into my selling area. Although their variety of ethnic foods is much less than mine, they are priced lower on certain key items. What I need to know is how loyal our customers are to our special services, including cooking demonstrations, taste-tests, and special ordering.

Personal Workshop Preparation #5: What's My Problem?

Personal Workshop #5 provides you an opportunity to describe some marketing problems you could use some help in solving.

In preparation for Personal Workshop #5, observe how case study entrepreneur Marie Nelson completed this workshop.

THE PURPOSE OF THIS WORKSHOP IS TO IDENTIFY TWO MARKETING PROBLEMS THAT YOU HAVE BEEN UNABLE TO SOLVE AND THEN DETAIL WHAT INFORMATION YOU FEEL YOU NEED TO SOLVE THEM.

Personal Workshop #5
What's My Problem?

Marketing Problem #1:

How to enter the corporate incentive gift market.

Marketing Problem #2:

How to enter the military exchange market.

Information Needed— Problem #1:

Identities of key intermediaries; a vehicle to introduce ourselves; statistics on first year financials for new products introduced; information on additional packaging and distribution costs expected.

Information Needed—Problem #2:

Which military agencies to approach and names of specific contact people; recommendations necessary to open doors; the contracting procedures used and the supplier documentation demanded.

Personal Workshop #5
What's My Problem?

Marketing Problem #1:

Marketing Problem #2:

Information Needed— Problem #1:

Information Needed—Problem #2:

Workshop Follow-Up

1. Often the most postponed step in market research is defining the problem. But if you really think about it, you know what the problems are—just not the solutions yet. This workshop guides you to define the problem.

2. Once you define the problem you can use your existing resources, including other customers, your suppliers, your banker, etc. to define what information you need to solve the problem. Once you know what information you need, you are ready to perform some market research.

Types of Research

Informal Research

Business owner/managers can collect marketing information in a variety of ways. The method can often be quite simple—no crystal ball or advanced degree is required. Consider the example of a restaurant that encourages patrons to drop their business cards in a fish bowl as they leave. This simple practice can help the restaurant understand its market area.

Restaurant patrons drop their business cards in the fish bowl for a chance to win a free lunch in a weekly drawing. That free lunch is a small price for the restaurant to pay for all the market information in the fish bowl. For starters, those cards provide the eatery with:

- customers' names

- titles

- employers

- addresses

- phone numbers

Of what use is this information? The addresses show how far customers come to eat lunch there. The restaurant owner can use those addresses to construct a map of his or her market area and to decide where to place advertising. He or she might choose a billboard ad in the middle of that area or an ad in a bus that runs nearby. The owner could produce flyers or coupons to distribute in office complexes where customers work.

Tracking Down Customer Information

As you can see, gathering information about your market can be both simple and valuable. There are several key sources of information on your customers:

Checks and Sales Receipts. Using customers' addresses and zip codes or a street map, owner/managers can:

- figure out how far customers travel to shop at their business

- get clues about their income and lifestyles

- use those clues to pinpoint what goods and services to provide

  - base advertising decisions on this information:

  - where to place outdoor ads

  - which newspapers to use

  - which radio and TV stations will best reach customers

- use customer addresses in a mailing list for direct mail brochures or for coupon offers hung on doorknobs

Businesses such as service stations and car repair shops can find out a lot about customers from their license plate numbers. If their state won't provide addresses based on license numbers, businesses can obtain that information from R. L. Polk & Company of Detroit, Michigan, for a small fee.

Credit Records. Addresses are listed, along with the customers' occupations and income. These and other outlets of information can help business owners to measure their customers' interests and ability to purchase certain products and to figure out which promotional tactics will work best.

Complaint Records. Most businesses have some form of recording customer complaints. Any customer report of problems should be taken seriously as a matter of good business. As a source of marketing information, complaints can point out:

- service problems
- poor quality products
- gaps in inventory
- inconveniences in business layout, location or parking

Customer Questions and Suggestions. Customers don't just contact a business to complain. Sometimes they have questions about a product or service. They may have a suggestion. Some may even want to praise a product or employee for a job well done. These customer contacts also are good sources of marketing information.

Employees. Casual conversations with workers can provide a realistic insight into the business. Especially if they work with customers every day, employees can point out pluses and problems.

Customers. In addition to the information they gain from asking customers what they like and don't like about the business, owner/managers can build goodwill. Customers like to know that a business owner values and appreciates their opinions.

- **People watching**. Business owner/managers can observe:
  - how old their customers are
  - how many shop with children
  - what types of customers shop at different times of the day
  - age of customers
  - estimated income level of customers
  - profession of customers
  - other benchmarks

Secondary Research

Secondary research or data refers to information collected by someone else and available in published form. It may be found in books, periodicals or on-line computer databases.

For starters, secondary information is easily available. Tracking it down can be as easy as stopping by the library. It's inexpensive. And it may save time and money by providing data business owners might otherwise have to collect on their own. On the other hand, if someone else collected the information to help solve their marketing problems, it may take some patience to find information that applies directly to your business.

Where do you start? The public library or, better yet, a nearby college or university library is bound to offer some helpful data. The best bet is a specialized business school library at a larger university.

Several publications are good general references to start an information search:

- *Business Periodical Index* (**BPI**) is a guide to articles published in the business press on various topics. It includes such general publications as *Business Week, The Wall Street Journal, Forbes* and *Fortune*. The BPI also includes references in such trade or industry publications as *Advertising Age, Chain Store Age* and *Progressive Grocer.*

- **Computer version of the** *Business Periodical Index.* Users type in key words that summarize their topic of interest, so researchers must zero in on what they want to find out and why. The more specific key words are, the better. General terms are likely to turn up so many references that they will overwhelm the researcher.

- *Standard Industrial Classification (SIC) Manual*, published by the U.S. Department of Commerce, also can point researchers in the right direction for information on businesses and their markets. A short course on the SIC coding system is in order here. SIC codes direct researchers to industry information starting with two digits. The more specific the information available, the more digits will turn up.

    20   Food Products

    202   Dairy Products

    2022   Cheese

- **Census Bureau**. The largest publisher of data in the United States, the Census Bureau provides data not only on regional population characteristics, but also on business and economic activity. Business owners might find valuable information on competitors, customers and market area by examining such publications as the *Census of Housing, Census of Service Industries, Census of Retail Trade* and *Census of Manufacturers*.

- **State and Local Government Agencies** also publish information on business activity and trends. State commerce and development departments frequently conduct studies aimed at attracting new business; that information often is available to the public. Local planning commissions and downtown redevelopment groups publish similar reports. Chambers of commerce provide information about the community and its businesses.

- The *Encyclopedia of Associations* is a multi-volume set of reference guides which list every known trade association in the U.S. with address, phone number and a description of its activities. A call to a trade association librarian can yield very useful information.

- **Computer databases such as CompuServe, Dow Jones and Dialog** are among available databases that researchers can access via computer modem. Because databases usually charge by the minute, its is best to narrow down your search before your start. If, for instance, a researcher requests information on "retail advertising," the response could well be overwhelming—and expensive. Narrowing the search down to a specific business will cut expensive search time and provide only the most pertinent data.

Primary Research

While informal information collection and secondary data is useful, this type of market research may not always provide the answers you need. The next step is primary research, the collection of new data to provide information specific to your business.

Key Words

Primary data collection takes two forms. **Quantitative research** usually involves asking structured questions, often in questionnaire form, to large groups of people and using statistics to draw conclusions. **Qualitative research**, on the other hand, involves small groups in an informal, unstructured setting.

Qualitative Research

Qualitative methods may provide all the marketing research a business needs. But they are also used as a prelude to more formal, quantitative techniques.

FYI

Focus group members typically receive compensation for their time, anywhere from a meal or a small gift to hundreds of dollars, depending on the length and purpose of the session. Given this practice, marketing researchers are wise to screen focus group members to weed out "professional respondents." Asking potential respondents if they have participated in any research in the last three months should effectively screen the services of an experienced moderator. The moderator's job is to make sure that all respondents voice their opinions and that they speak to the subject at hand.

For example, a business may form a focus group to help construct a formal questionnaire. Qualitative research also is used to help a business measure its customers needs and interests. For example, the idea for hand soap in a pump dispenser evolved from informal research sessions in which homemakers expressed dismay with messy bar soaps and suggested liquid soap in an easy dispenser.

> *"The common facts of today are the products of yesterday's research."*
>
> —Duncan MacDonald

- **Focus groups** are the most common method of qualitative research. A typical focus group brings together 6 to 12 customers, usually from similar backgrounds, to discuss a specific topic. Their conversation is guided by a moderator whose job is to focus attention on the topic. An informal setting and tone help elicit frank opinions. Focus groups typically are recorded on either video or audio tape.

  A major advantage of focus groups is that respondents can say what they want instead of just answering "yes" or "no" to a survey. That's why many businesses use focus groups to determine which questions to ask in quantitative research. Many surveys make the mistake of assuming the questions asked cover the issues that most concern customers.

The Do's and Don'ts of Focus Groups

- Focus groups are not flawless. Because they involve only a handful of people, their responses may not represent the majority of customers. Businesses considering major marketing decisions shouldn't depend just on focus groups for their research. And businesses should take care in recruiting focus group members.

- To encourage participation, the safest bet is to find respondents similar in age and background. An elderly woman, for instance, might be hesitant to speak up in a group dominated by college students. If the goal is to seek diverse opinions, forming several focus groups might be a better option.

- Focus groups often end up with at least one know-it-all. That's when the service of an experienced moderator pays off. The moderator's job is to make sure that all respondents voice their opinions and that they speak to the subject at hand.

A more economical option may be to contact the marketing department of the business school in a nearby college or university. The department may even offer to conduct that research for a business at little or no cost as a class project.

FYI

Business owner/managers can conduct their own focus groups as long as they are honest in their ability to remain objective about what is being said. Otherwise the process of recruiting respondents, holding and recording the session, and interpreting the responses is best left to professionals. Most marketing research firms listed in the yellow pages routinely run focus groups. Advertising agencies also may have experience in conducting focus groups.

Quantitative Research

While qualitative research can provide valuable insights, those findings may not apply to all customers. When a business wants a more representative viewpoint, quantitative research is the tool to use.

Quantitative research gathers information through a survey administered to many respondents. The three most common survey methods are:

- telephone interviews
- mail surveys
- personal interviews

Each has advantages and disadvantages.

Telephone Surveys

The most common method, primarily because phone numbers are readily accessible and/or random dialing is easy. Another advantage is that surveyors can pick up a good deal of information from respondents in a short time.

However, telephone interviews have their drawbacks. Even though people naturally answer a ringing phone, they can easily end the survey by hanging up. Respondents may not be home when a surveyor calls, or they may be using their answering machine to screen calls.

Pros and Cons of Telephone Surveys

Advantages

- Flexibility
- Speed of results
- Broad and quick geographic coverage
- Low cost

Disadvantages

- Time limitations (the survey must be short)
- No visual aids allowed
- Limited duration
- Question limitations

If surveyors use the phone book to track down respondents, they'll miss clients with unlisted numbers. That may sound like a minor problem, but leaving out families with unpublished numbers can skew phone survey results. In such cities as Las Vegas and Los Angeles, more than half of all phone numbers are unlisted. Even in smaller cities like Flint, Michigan, a third of all households choose not to publish their phone numbers.

Mail Surveys

About a fourth of all marketing research is conducted through the mail. Researchers use mailing lists either compiled from company records or purchased from specialized companies. A major advantage of mail surveys is low cost.

The biggest disadvantage of mail surveys is a relatively low response rate: the number of surveys mailed compared to the number returned. Often a second mailing of the survey is needed to boost the response rate. Another disadvantage is the lack of control over who completes the survey. If researchers want to reach the family member who normally does the grocery shopping, they can ask for that person in a phone call. But in a mailed questionnaire, they can't be certain who filled out the form.

Pros and Cons of Mail Surveys

Advantages

- Easier and more inexpensive than telephone or personal interviews
- More efficient for larger samples
- Best access to hard-to-reach respondents
- Less interviewer bias (though the questions or sequence may reflect bias of author(s))

Disadvantages

- Often require second mailing to be effective
- Low rate of return
- No control over who completes survey

Personal Interviews

Face-to-face meetings with a purpose. They differ from informal chats with customers because they are planned and organized. Without planning, interviews are just "talking with the folks."

In personal interviews, surveyors follow a set list of questions in the form of either a questionnaire or an interview guide. Which form your survey should take depends on the interviewer's experience and the purpose of the survey. The more experienced interviewers are, the better equipped they are to "wing it" with a guide. But a questionnaire can be phrased to sound like spoken words, allowing the survey to avoid a stilted feel and at the same time eliminate potential interviewer bias.

Pros and Cons of Personal Interviews

Advantages

- Flexibility (the specifics of the interview are likely to change after the first few interviews)
- Ability to catch and correct confusing or seemingly contradictory statements
- Potential to gather more detailed information

- Ability to display pictures, videos or actual products
- Benefit of interviewers observing responses
- Increased participation by respondents
- Opportunity to probe for additional information

Disadvantages
- More costly than mail or telephone surveys
- Outcome dependent on interviewers with good sales skills

Surveying a Sample

Key Word

The group of respondents an interviewer surveys is called a **sample**. Surveys aim to reach a sample whose opinions reflect those of the company's target market(s). Business owner/managers must answer this question:

Are the opinions of these respondents close enough to those of our customers' that we can base a sound business decision on this survey?

Many people are skeptical of the concept that a small sample of respondents can mirror the opinions of a mass audience. They look askance at television networks that claim to project election winners after polling only 500 or so voters. How can accurate prediction be based on so few opinions? All the media does is poll the voting preference of a sample.

These examples illustrate how sampling works. You decide to take a swim on a hot August afternoon. But before you jump in, you want to know how cold the water is. You dip your foot in the pool to test it. You don't need to dive in and swim to the other end to know the water is freezing. All you need is a sample.

The same principle holds true for the pasta cook who needn't test every string of spaghetti to see if they're done; one or two pieces will do.

FYI

To select your sample size, be aware that in general terms, if 100 people respond to a survey and half of them answer one question the same way, a business owner can be 90 percent certain that the sample represents the target group. If half of a 500-respondent survey answers one question the same way, the degree of certainty is 95 percent. Of course, increasing the sample from 100 to 500 takes a lot more time and effort.

A safe guideline is that each subgroup to be analyzed should have a minimum of 100 units. Therefore if a survey's goal is to measure the opinions of three subgroups and experience predicts a five percent survey return, a business would need to mail out 6,000 surveys

Sampling is a practical alternative to a census, in which every member of a group is questioned. Sampling is quicker and cheaper than a census, and it holds a safe degree of certainty that the opinions of the sample reflect those of the group.

There are three steps involved in surveying your sample:

1. Determine which group the survey aims to represent. If the business is an auto parts store, the group probably will be people who do their own car repairs.

2. Figure out what size sample will provide enough responses on which to base marketing decisions. The rule is that the larger the sample, the more confidence a business can have that those opinions reflect the group's. Time, money and the survey method tend to dictate how many respondents surveyors can reach.

3. Decide whether to use a probability or nonprobability sample. Nonprobability samples do not allow the calculation of probabilities that the findings are correct within a certain known range of error. Nonprobability samples are often used for exploratory, or "quick and dirty," research.

The basic types of nonprobability samples are:

- *Judgment samples*, in which business owner/managers use their own judgment to choose who to sample (they might, for instance, choose to sample experts in their industry);

- *Convenience samples*, which targets the most convenient respondents; and

- *Quota samples*, which ensure that various population subgroups are represented on pertinent sample characteristics, such as age, employment or income.

Probability sampling is more scientific and objective. The sample is selected at random, and everyone has an equal and known chance of being selected. To select a probability sample, surveyors must have a list for the entire population. The main types of probability samples are:

- *Random samples*, in which each member of the population has an equal chance of being included in the sample (surveyors may pull names from a hat, for instance, or use a random number table to select names from the list);

- *Stratified random samples,* which are drawn from a number of different subgroups to assure representation of each subgroup (drawing random samples from the paper industry and printing industry instead of one sample from both); and

- *Systematic sampling*, in which every "nth" name from the population is sampled. Surveyors start at a random spot, not the beginning or end of a sorted list. This method is easier to draw than a random sample.

Questionnaire Design

Imagine that a business has decided what survey method to use and how many respondents will form the right sample. Now all that company needs is survey questions.

Questionnaire construction is one of the most difficult steps in marketing research. Yet, many people seem to think putting together a good questionnaire is easy. That's why there are so many terrible questionnaires—full of confusing or incomprehensible questions all but guaranteed to produce worthless results. The format and outline of a typical questionnaire is described below.

The **screening question**, also known as the qualifying question, makes sure the respondent is the right person to answer the survey. These questions help phone and mall surveyors figure out if they're talking to a person who is part of the target group.

> *Example:* A surveyor for an auto parts store asks, "Have you done any of your own car repairs in the past six months?" If the answer is "yes," the survey continues. If not, the interviewer moves on to the next respondent.

The **introduction** lets respondents know who is conducting the survey and why. It lets respondents know what's in it for them.

> *Example:* a mail survey from an automobile manufacturer begins, "Your opinion of your BMW and your BMW dealership is important to us. Finding out what you think will help us meet your expectations—now and in the future."

Open-ended or closed-ended questions provide the substance of the survey.

Open-ended questions let respondents answer in their own words, guaranteeing a variety of responses, but making it difficult to categorize and analyze results.

> *Example:* What one thing could we have done today to make your food better?

Closed-ended questions give respondents a limited choice of answers.

> *Example:* Yes or no—Would you recommend your BMW dealership to a friend or relative?

> *Example:* Multiple choice questions—Which slogan do you prefer for Lotsafizz Soda? (select ONE)
>
> _____ Lotsafizz. The name says it all.
> _____ More bubbles for your buck.
> _____ It'll tickle your nose.

Example: Scaled-response questions—On a scale of 1 to 5, with 5 as the best rating, how did you like the movie you just saw?

1 2 3 4 5

Example: Scaled-response questions—Please indicate how much you like or dislike each brand of soda by placing a check in the appropriate space:

	Strongly Like	Like	Neither Like or Dislike	Dislike	Strongly Dislike
Coca-Cola	___	___	___	___	___
Lotsafizz	___	___	___	___	___
Pepsi	___	___	___	___	___
Dr. Pepper	___	___	___	___	___
7-UP	___	___	___	___	___

Example: Ranking questions—Please rank the following brands of sugar-free colas. Put number 1 for your first choice, 2 for your second choice, and so on.

Brand A _____
Brand B _____
Brand C _____
Brand D _____
Brand E _____

FYI

The most common pitfall in designing questionnaires is poorly worded questions. Unclear questions leave respondents puzzled and produce meaningless results of no help in marketing decisions. Here are some tips on writing clear questions that will elicit helpful responses:

• Consider the respondent's point of view. Keep questions simple and concise. Avoid jargon and technical terms.

• Ask one question at a time. "Double-barreled questions" seek two opinions at once, which is certain to confuse people. Example: "Was the service you received today quick and courteous?"

• Keep choices "mutually exclusive," so that answers fall into clear and separate categories.

• Avoid "loaded" questions that imply a correct answer. For example: "How frequently do you shop at lower class stores like the Dollar Store?"

• Keep it simple. Start with easier questions and gradually work into more difficult questions.

• Save personal questions for last.

Demographic questions cover age, income, marital status, education level, housing value, etc. This information allows a business to categorize responses and make sure the respondent fits the target group. These questions usually come last because they are personal, and some people are hesitant to answer.

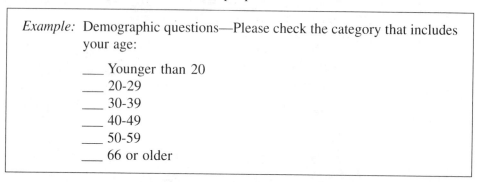

Example: Demographic questions—Please check the category that includes your age:

___ Younger than 20
___ 20-29
___ 30-39
___ 40-49
___ 50-59
___ 66 or older

Warning! Here is a simple rule for length of survey: the shorter, the better. Don't try to collect information just because it would be "nice to know."

Analyzing and Interpreting Research Results

The first step in analyzing primary data is "editing" questionnaires to make sure as many questionnaires as possible are usable. Editing involves checking to see if all questions are answered and all pages completed and if respondents took the survey seriously. In sum, the editing process assures that the data is present, consistent and accurate.

The next step is "coding," which assigns numerical values to responses so the answers can be assigned to groups. Coding also makes the data suitable for computer analysis.

In most cases, closed-ended questions are the easiest to precode before the survey so the data can be entered promptly in the computer. Open-ended questions usually must be postcoded, or assigned a value based on responses, before they can be analyzed.

After data has been collected, edited and coded, analysis begins as business owner/ managers assess responses from the survey sample. The simplest form of analysis takes the form of tabulation and graphs. These analyses are typically the first summaries of survey results.

Tabulation offers simple percentages of how the sample responded to questions. The simplest form of tabulation is called a *frequency distribution* or a one-way frequency table. It examines one question at a time. The following table indicates

FYI

Always pre-test a survey before presenting it to a larger group. Business owner/managers should ask a few people who reflect the desired sample to go through the survey and help work out any bugs.

the number of respondents who gave each possible answer to the question. See Table 1.1. Most research projects use computers to generate one-way frequency tables for each question, but some still work out frequency distributions by hand.

Table 1.1: A Frequency Distribution
Use of Automatic Teller Machine

	Value	Frequency	Percent	Cumulative Percent
No	0	39%	39%	39%
Yes	1	61%	61%	100%
Total	100	100%	100%	

Age	Value	Frequency	Percent	Cumulative Percent
18-34	1	22%	23%	23%
35-54	2	30%	32%	55%
55+	3	42%	45%	100%
Total	94	100%	100%	

The next step in data analysis is to compare responses from question to question. These *cross-tabulations*, or *cross-tabs*, are the core of many studies done for large corporations by major marketing research firms. Cross-tabs arrange response variables into rows and columns. See Table 1.2.

As an example of how to interpret row percent, you can see that of the number of people who responded 'no' (40 people), five percent (two people) were in the age group, 18 to 34. Of those who responded 'yes,' 37 percent were in the age group 18 to 34. As an example of column percent, you can see that of the people surveyed who were in the age group 18 to 34, (22 people), nine percent (two people) do not use Automated Teller Machines (ATMs). Ninety-one percent do use ATMs.

Table 1.2: A Cross-Tab Evaluation
Use of Automatic Teller Machine by Age

Count	Age 18-34	Age 35-54	Age 55+	Row Total
Use? - No	2	12	26	40
Row Percent	5%	30%	65%	
Column Percent	9%	40%	62%	
Total Percent	2%	13%	28%	43%
Use? - Yes	20	18	16	54
Row Percent	37%	33%	30%	
Column Percent	91%	60%	38%	
Total Percent	21%	19%	17%	57%
Column	22	30	42	94
Total	23%	32%	45%	100%

Cross-tabs are a powerful, efficient and easily understood way to summarize results. However, they analyze only two variables at time, so that one questionnaire can generate a huge number of possible cross-tabs. Data must be selected with care to produce meaningful results.

Charts and graphs also can make survey results easier to comprehend. A variety of computer programs can help create useful graphs with a minimum of effort.

A pie chart (as shown in Figure 1.1) denotes the percentages of a frequency distribution as slices of a circle or "pie." A bar chart (see Figure 1.2) compares percentages of a frequency distribution using side-by-side bars. Both methods present data in a flexible, easily understood way.

**Figure 1.1:A Pie Chart
ATM Users by Age**

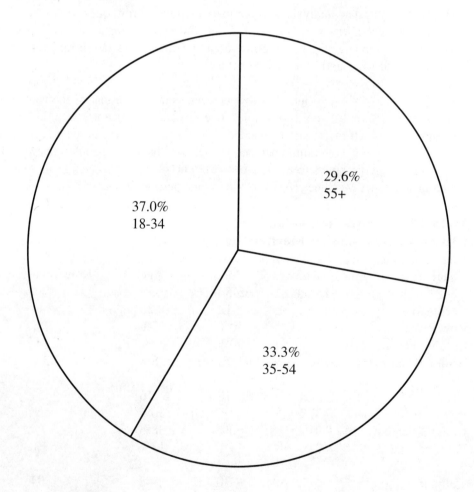

Figure 1.2: A Bar Chart
ATM Users by Age

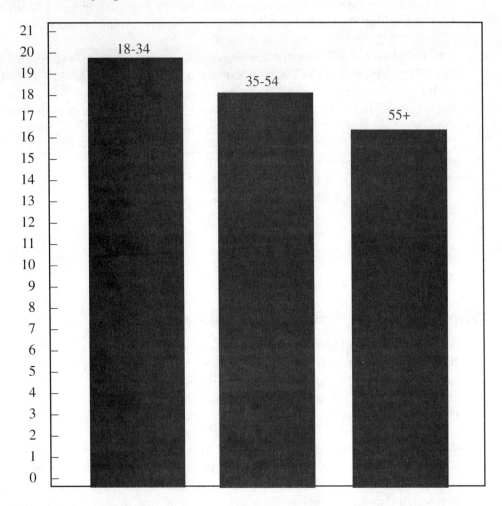

Frequency distributions, cross-tabs and graphs can help lay out survey results, but sometimes these statistics are not enough. Suppose, for instance, that a business wants to compare its service with a competitor's. It could draw up a frequency distribution, like the one shown in Table 1.3, to compare the percentage of people who rated the business and its competition above average.

Table 1.3: Service Comparison by Percentage

Rating	Us	Competition
5	25%	22%
4	18%	27%
3	40%	34%
2	7%	9%
1	10%	8%

The range of percentages represented in Table 1.3 (p. 41) makes it difficult to identify which business earns the higher rating. The business has a higher percentage of five ratings than its competition, but a lower percentage of four ratings. Adding up the percentages of five, four and three ratings make it a draw.

The business could determine the mean value to help clarify the results as shown in Table 1.4. To calculate the mean, a business must add the values of each response and divide by the number of responses. Table 1.4 indicates that the business and its competitor are running fairly even in terms of service ratings.

Table 1.4: Service Comparison by Average Rating		
	Us	**Competition**
Mean	3.41	3.46

Where To Find Research Assistance

By now you probably realize how much marketing research can benefit your business. And much of it you can do yourself. But for some special projects, you may be thinking, "There's no way I can do this myself!" Don't worry. That's a common reaction. For business owner/managers considering focus groups or a large-group survey, marketing specialists can help put a research project together.

Who can you turn to for marketing research help? If your business employs an advertising agency, that's a good starting point. A major advantage of working with your ad agency is that the people there already know your business and its needs, and they want to keep your account. Even if your agency doesn't specialize in the type of research you need, its staff probably can refer you to a firm that can provide that expertise.

If you don't employ an advertising agency, you may want to track down a marketing research firm to undertake your project. The yellow pages in most cities list these firms and outline what services they offer. Some marketing research firms are full-service; they can provide all types of studies and analysis. Others specialize in, say, focus groups or phone surveys.

FYI

An excellent, inexpensive guide to performing your own marketing research is the publication from the U.S. Small Business Administration, *Researching Your Market,* Item #MT08. To order: contact SBA Publications, PO Box 46521, Denver, CO 80201-0030.

Business schools at colleges and universities often have Small Business Institutes or Small Business Development Centers which can provide you with assistance. College professors also can offer assistance, and some might take on a research effort as a class project at little or no cost to the business. The best bet is to call the business school at a nearby university and ask to speak with the professors who teach market research.

You Have Completed Challenge 1

Challenge 1 has given you the opportunity to take a break from your hectic daily marketing activities to stand back and examine your strategy to attract customers. The key question you should answer is: Does our current marketing strategy encourage us to think like our customers?

Additional questions you should answer include: Do we regularly solicit customer comments and suggestions? How do we use this valuable input to improve our ability to anticipate our customers' needs? How well do we balance our financial needs and our desire to sell to a wide variety of customers? Are we able to tell what it really costs to supply each customer? Do we truly understand our niche in the marketplace?

If you are unable to answer each of these questions convincingly, you may find it useful to design and conduct additional market research. In Challenge 1 you have also learned, in detail, about the different types of market research available and how to design cost-effective research projects. You have also seen how the results of a variety of market research techniques are commonly interpreted. The hopeful outcome is your increased comfort in considering your customers' part in your marketing team. Once you adopt this mentality, you open yourself to drawing upon the tremendous imagination and creativity that your customers are pleased to share with you.

You Leave Challenge 1 with the Following

Information: You have the knowledge to plan a systematic approach to evaluating your selection of customers in light of your company's needs for dependable revenue, current market information and access to important decision-makers in your industry.

Tools: The Personal Workshops are evaluation tools designed to help you better understand what your customers are thinking and how well your current marketing programs fulfill their needs and wants.

Learning: You have been introduced to market-tested techniques for small business marketing that can help you compete in today's business world.

Networking: You have been given resources for conducting exploratory market research, examining existing sources of market facts and opinions and performing highly detailed market surveys to provide customized information uniquely required by your company's marketing strategy.

Challenge 1: Self-Assessment

As an action-oriented business owner, you most likely want to prove to yourself that you have understood the concepts and techniques presented in Challenge 1 sufficiently well so that you can make an immediate positive impact on your company's marketing.

The following self-assessment guides you through a checklist of questions and activities to permit you to complete a personalized "reality check."

PART ONE: Fundamentals of Small Business Marketing
Evaluating Your Customer's Satisfaction

**Pages
2 - 7**

( ) I can identify in detail the three most important customer benefits of my product or service

( ) I can detail in writing how my marketing delivers customer satisfaction better than my competition

( ) I can explain why a sales prospect should believe that we are a reliable supplier

( ) I can identify what we have done in the past year to make ordering from us more convenient for our customers

What Makes Effective Marketing

**Pages
7 - 12**

( ) I know how much we spent on marketing in the past year

( ) I can explain what specific marketing projects we undertook in the past year and what the sales results were of each program

( ) I can present in a concise, persuasive form our company's basic marketing message

( ) I can detail how we integrate our marketing message and visual design in all of our marketing communication pieces

( ) I can elaborate on our training plan to assure consistent knowledge of our marketing programs by all employees

Being Market-Driven

( ) I can explain how we have used market research in the past year to better define our customers' needs

( ) I can directly relate our product/service features to documented customer needs

( ) I can describe what techniques we use to regularly solicit customer suggestions for improvements in our product/service design and our marketing programs

**Pages
12 - 16**

( ) I can explain how we maintain detailed customer records, including past complaints, suggestions and order patterns

Selecting Your Customers

( ) I can describe which customers produce the majority of our sales

( ) I can describe how often our key customers ordered in the past year

( ) I can detail a plan to stimulate at least one additional order per year per customer

**Pages
16 - 23**

( ) I can explain how we use our customer relationships to learn how to better use new technology, skills and technical knowledge

( ) I can describe which of our customers are "knowledge rich"

( ) I can detail what communication methods we use to stay in touch with our key customers

PART TWO: Do-It-Yourself Market Research
Creating and Executing a Customized
Market Research Plan

( ) I can define one or more marketing problems we feel we need additional information to solve

( ) I can detail what ongoing market research we conduct and describe each method

**Pages
24 - 43**

( ) I can demonstrate my understanding of the effective use of specific market research techniques such as focus groups and questionnaire design

RECORD ANYTHING FROM
CHALLENGE 1, YOUR PERSONAL
WORKSHOPS, OR YOUR
PERSONAL REFLECTIONS THAT
YOU WANT TO REMEMBER.

Take Another Look

Review the results of your Challenge 1 Self-Assessment. Which areas do you still need to work on? Follow up on these areas by reviewing appropriate sections of the Challenge.

Challenge 2
Frugal Marketing Planning

"The plan is nothing, planning is everything."

–Eisenhower

A re you making the most of your marketing dollar?

All businesses, from the large corporation to the solely-owned and operated small business, need a plan to direct their future actions and make the most of scarce marketing resources. Too much is at stake to simply think that everything is going to fall in place, your competitors are not going to react, or that everyone in your business will intuitively understand the path you're taking. Planning is the only way to assure that you are making the most of the resources that you commit to marketing.

Challenge 1 of this course discussed the importance of the perceptions that you and your customers have of your business and offered direction for gaining information about the marketplace. Challenge 2 explores how to lay the foundation for your marketing plan. You will begin by looking at how a marketing plan can help your business.

Upon completion of Challenge 2 you will be able to:

- Build your marketing plan on a strong foundation

- Conduct a situation analysis

- Define your target markets

- Estimate your market demand

- Assess your competition

- Analyze your own company's strengths and weaknesses

- Set SMART objectives

- Develop and implement strategies and tactics

What Is a Marketing Plan?

A marketing plan is a guide, much like a blueprint guides a builder or a chart guides a pilot. It shows where you are now, where you want to end up, and a route to get you to your destination.

47

Can you imagine a builder starting to build a house without plans? Designing rooms, buying material, scheduling workers, all without thinking ahead? What do you think that house would look like? Would you want to buy it? How many other people do you think would want to buy one of his houses?

What about an airline pilot who flies her plane to a location that she has never been, who departs without checking her aircraft, charts, or weather forecasts. Would you want to be a passenger on her plane?

What about a small business manager who opens the doors of his business every day without really knowing who his customers are, what their preferences are or without a plan to guide the business's mix of products and services, prices, promotions and distribution concerns. Would you want to invest in this business? Would you want to work for someone without a plan?

No! Yet most small businesses operate this way.

We would probably call the builder arrogant and wasteful. Imagine the idea of building a house without asking potential homeowners what they want in their home! Besides meeting the size and appearance needs of a buyer, there is bound to be added expenses in scheduling workers when there is no work to be done. What about wasted materials he would end up with by building without a plan? We would probably call the builder unemployed.

We would probably call the pilot careless and irresponsible. Think of the risks of flying without knowing where you were headed, where other aircraft were or if you were approaching dangerous weather. We would probably call the pilot grounded.

But what about the small business manager operating without a marketing plan? What would you call him? **Typical.**

Why should a small business manager be any different from the builder or pilot? In reality he's not. We could probably use the same terms we used for the builder and pilot in describing him.

"The will to win is nothing unless you have the will to prepare."

—Anonymous

The marketing plan is simply a well thought-out, written document that outlines how you intend to achieve your goals. A good foundation is laid by analyzing where you are and what is happening around you. Specific and measurable objectives are set. Strategies and action plans to achieve those objectives are developed. And finally a plan to monitor progress is put in place.

Why You Need a Marketing Plan

Why should someone invest their efforts in planning?

Some managers may think they are too busy running the business to spend any of their important time on planning activities. At the other extreme is the manager who produces a great plan and then files it away, never to take any action to implement his or her thoughts. Of course, these examples are the extremes. A business can realize several valuable benefits by developing a marketing plan.

Planning forces decision makers to identify the firm's strengths and weaknesses, and opportunities and threats. As a result, the manager is in a position to capitalize on the strengths and address the weaknesses. Developing a plan forces a manager to develop direction and objectives for the business to accomplish. The process requires a manager to establish priorities and to think through the proposed actions and consequences. Tracking the plan ensures that strategies will be developed to address weaknesses. A marketing plan helps focus team efforts and specific tactics to be followed, including:

> *"Make preparation in advance. You never have trouble if you are prepared for it."*
>
> —Teddy Roosevelt

- what strategies will be implemented

- who is responsible for various tasks

- when each task should be completed and

- what resources will be needed to complete the task

An additional benefit is the information it conveys about your competitive environment and objectives to yourself, your employees, new employees or outsiders who may have a financial interest in your company.

Although the benefits of a marketing plan seem obvious, many managers may still choose to operate without them. Like the builder without a plan and the pilot without a chart, these managers place a great deal of their future on chance, fate or just plain luck. The intent of this Challenge is to help you develop the foundation for a marketing plan that will ultimately guide your business to accomplishing your objectives.

Why Some Marketing Plans May Fail

Possessing a marketing plan is not a guarantee of success. Nothing is a substitute for good managerial decision making. Remember, if you do not achieve all your objectives, don't take it as a sign of failure or poor planning. Quite the contrary, that is what planning is all about. Review the basis for your decisions. Adjust your plans. Begin the next cycle in the planning process.

Some plans, however, have a greater likelihood of success than others. Common problems with plans may include the following:

> *"Genius is one percent inspiration and ninety-nine percent perspiration."*
>
> —Thomas Edison

Lack of an Adequate Situation Analysis: The situation analysis is the foundation for the entire plan. Lacking vital information on your own business or on your competitors may result in short-sighted plans. Remember the old adage, "Garbage in, garbage out." Take time to do your homework. To save you time in the **long run**, the situation analysis should be an **on-going** activity, not something reserved just for planning time.

Paradise Potions, Jim Copeland: I keep a file folder where I place any information I find on food trends. This includes articles from trade publications relating to sales trends, articles from consumer magazines describing the latest fads, and tidbits of information I receive from the wholesalers who sell my products. I use this information as a source of ideas for new products. I also use this information to try to predict the future popularity of our flavored dips, salsas, and sauces.

> *"It's not enough to be industrious; so are the ants. What are you industrious about?"*
>
> —Henry David Thoreau

Unrealistic Objectives: Don't underestimate or overestimate your objectives or goals; either typically results in poor follow through by all involved.

Not Enough Details: Your objectives may be fine but your strategy and the steps to implement it may not be complete. Make sure you didn't make too many assumptions that tasks would be completed without assigning a deadline and responsibility.

Status Quo: Your strategies are the same as last year, yet you expect different results.

Plan not Implemented: Often the plan is written and placed in a file. Without action, planning is a waste of time. Specific action plans which tell what tasks are to be completed, when and by whom are necessary to assure implementation.

Unanticipated Competitor Actions: The sign of good competition is swift and decisive action on their part. Don't underestimate your competitors. Leave yourself enough leeway to adjust your plans and budgets.

Progress is not Evaluated: The only way to fine tune your plan is to evaluate what works and what doesn't. It doesn't matter if you do things right if you are doing the wrong things.

Many of the characteristics needed for a successful marketing plan are highlighted throughout this Challenge. One last suggestion should be mentioned. Make sure that your plan is flexible. A flexible plan will allow you to make changes as your resources shift, your competitors react, and the environment evolves. Use your marketing plan as a guide to help you achieve your goals.

Le Caribe Wholesalers, Marie Nelson: I keep a file folder of complaints from my sales force and my customers. I have one file folder for general complaints that I use to make improvements to the service we provide to customers. I also have a file folder for each of our competitors. Every time a sale is lost to that competitor, I place a note in the file detailing why the food store selected the competitor.

An Overview of a Marketing Plan

A marketing plan has three major sections, a *situation analysis*, an *objective section* and a *strategy and action plan*. The first set, *the situation analysis*, describes the current business environment. It answers the questions "Where are we?" and " Where are we going?" By answering these questions, decision makers identify and examine factors that affect their business. Using the information compiled in the situation analysis, the second section focuses on where the firm is headed, namely, its *objectives*. The objectives answer the question "What do we want to do?" Priorities must be established to direct the allocation of personnel, effort and resources. The final section, *the strategy and action plan,* outlines the marketing strategies that will be implemented and the specific actions that will be needed to implement those strategies and accomplish each objective, thus answering the questions, "How do we get where we want to go?"; "When do we want to arrive?"; "Who is responsible?"; and "How much will it cost?"

> *"Insanity is doing the same thing over and over and expecting different results."*

Marketing Plan		
Section 1	*Section 2*	*Section 3*
Situation	Writing	Developing
Analysis	Marketing	Strategies and
	Objectives	Action Plans

All of this sounds like a lot of information. A good marketing plan helps organize many of the thoughts and ideas that you think of regularly. Keep in mind the fact that when you completed some of the market research you were already beginning a planning process.

The Marketing Plan: The Situation Analysis

The situation analysis focuses on the business environment as it exists today. A large number of factors have an effect on your business. The purpose of this

FYI

The easiest way to evaluate progress is the tick mark method. Place a chart by each telephone or cash register. Then whenever a nonregular customer comes is, ask what encouraged him or her to come in. Place a tick mark next to the promotion that drew them in.

Promotion	Count
Newspaper ad	
Radio ad	
Direct mail	
Referred by a friend	

analysis is to help identify and concentrate your attention on the key variables that impact your business. Using this information as a starting point will help you steer your business toward its future goals.

The next series of workshops will help you develop the situation analysis for your business. The situation analysis is organized into four segments:

- Assessing Your Environment (Workshop 6).
- Focusing on your Most Likely Customers (Workshops 7, 8, 9, and 10).
- Assessing Your Competition (Workshops 11 and 12).
- Looking at Your Business (Workshops 13 and 14).

Assessing Your Environment

Marketing activities don't occur in a vacuum, but in an environment rich with many uncontrollable variables. These variables include regulations and laws, social attitudes, economic conditions, technological factors, and competitive factors. An important aspect of marketing is identifying opportunities and exploiting them. Market opportunities are the result of changes in the marketing environment. A successful marketer is aware of the environment and impending changes and able to determine how his or her business can capitalize on them. Without knowledge of the factors in the marketing environment, a manager may be like the pilot flying into the clouds, not knowing what lies ahead.

> *"The right information at the right time is nine-tenths of any battle."*
>
> —Napoleon

Personal Workshop Preparation #6: Assessing the Competition

By completing this marketing workshop, you will have a clear picture of the environment in which you operate. You will find the information you collect here a valuable resource when you are setting objectives and prioritizing strategies. Begin by getting the information in your head and your key employees' heads down on paper. Then determine if there are gaps you need to fill in by

FYI

Analyze the Situation

Assessing your environment
- Economic
- Political
- Psychological
- Legal
- Social
- Technological
- Ecological

Focusing on your most likely customers
- Who is your target market?
- What are customers needs and wants?
- How profitable is the market?

Assessing your competition
- Who are your competitors?
- What are their strengths and weaknesses?
- Why do customers buy from them?

Looking at your business
- Strengths
- Weaknesses
- Opportunities

gathering information already published. Your sources of information will be newspapers, trade magazines, and trade associations. Many of these sources can be uncovered in the reference section of your public library.

As a preview of the next workshop, observe how case study entrepreneur Marie Nelson, from Le Caribe Wholesalers, completed the exercise.

THE PURPOSE OF THIS WORKSHOP IS TO PROVIDE YOU WITH AN UNDERSTANDING OF THE ENVIRONMENTAL VARIABLES THAT IMPACT THE SUCCESS OF YOUR BUSINESS : TO UNCOVER POTENTIAL OPPORTUNITIES FOR YOUR BUSINESS; TO UNCOVER POTENTIAL THREATS TO YOUR BUSINESS.

Personal Workshop #6
Assessing The Environment

Economic

What is going to happen to the economy over the next six months? Next year?

The economy may slow down slightly in the next 6 months. If the Fed does not ease up on the interest rates, a mild recession is expected in the next year.

How will this impact your business?

In recessionary times, consumers spend less and retailers try to improve their profit margins. Offering specials to the retailers might help. Another strategy that might help is to assist retailers in keeping their costs down by helping them to better manage their inventory. Suggesting that retailers position themselves more strongly against restaurants may also be useful.

Political/Legal

What laws do you currently have to comply with?

Laws to be complied with include packaging and labeling laws, pricing laws such as the Robinson Patman Act, and promotional rules as governed by the FTC.

What changes are likely to occur in legislation that affects your business (i.e., pollution control, equal employment opportunity, product safety, advertising, price controls, etc.)?

No new legislation is likely.

Social/Psychological

What cultural trends will have an impact on the demand for your product or service?

The trend of eating ethnic foods seems to be strengthening. Also the trend toward easy and quick to prepare foods is growing.

What new trends can you capitalize on?

Keep track of the introduction of new cuisines on both the East Coast and the West Coast. These trends will catch on soon in the six-state market area.

Demographic

What are the demographic trends (i.e., age, income, gender, ethnicity, family size, occupation, education, etc.) that may alter the composition of your customer base?

The Baby Boomers are aging. Generation X is the next market to focus on.

What is the likely impact of these changes on your business?

As the Baby Boomers age, the desire for spicy foods may wane. The Generation Xers want things right now so convenience foods become more important.

Technological

How will new technologies affect the need for your product/service?

New technologies make the preparation of meals faster and easier. Therefore, focusing on products which can be prepared using the latest technologies is important.

How will new technologies affect the way your product/service is distributed?

With the use of the computer today, Le Caribe can keep track of the inventory sold by each store, so the sales force can be in the right place at the right time. Le Caribe can also analyze the product mix purchased by each store, thus aiding the sales force to cross-sell additional products.

How will new technologies affect the way your product/service is marketed?

Providing retailers with a fax machine may eliminate some labor in taking orders, as well as eliminating mistakes. It would also allow retailers to place orders 24 hours per day.

How will new technologies affect the way your product/service is produced?

As a wholesaler, Le Caribe does not produce any products.

Environmental

What is the environmental impact of producing or distributing your product?

Distribution of these food products has very little impact on the environment.

THE PURPOSE OF THIS WORKSHOP IS TO PROVIDE YOU WITH AN UNDERSTANDING OF THE ENVIRONMENTAL VARIABLES THAT IMPACT THE SUCCESS OF YOUR BUSINESS : TO UNCOVER POTENTIAL OPPORTUNITIES FOR YOUR BUSINESS; TO UNCOVER POTENTIAL THREATS TO YOUR BUSINESS.

Personal Workshop #6
Assessing The Environment

Economic

What is going to happen to the economy over the next six months? Next year?

How will this impact your business?

Political/Legal

What laws do you currently have to comply with?

What changes are likely to occur in legislation that affects your business (i.e., pollution control, equal employment opportunity, product safety, advertising, price controls, etc.)?

Social/Psychological

What cultural trends will have an impact on the demand for your product or service?

What new trends can you capitalize on?

Demographic

What are the demographic trends (i.e., age, income, gender, ethnicity, family size, occupation, education, etc.) that may alter the composition of your customer base?

What is the likely impact of these changes on your business?

Technological

How will new technologies affect the need for your product/service?

How will new technologies affect the way your product/service is distributed?

How will new technologies affect the way your product/service is marketed?

How will new technologies affect the way your product/service is produced?

Environmental

What is the environmental impact of producing or distributing your product?

Workshop Follow-Up

 1. Think about the effect the economy has on the demand for your product or service and adjust your marketing plan accordingly.

 2. Uncover trends that may indicate future opportunities or threats.

 3. Determine how technology will affect the demand for your product or service and affect the way you market.

Focusing on Your Most Likely Customers

In Challenge 1 you began to think like your customers. You began the process of selecting your customers by looking at how customers can help you even out your income flow, upgrade your skills and respond to business changes. Now that you have evaluated what types of customers you would like to work with, it is time to define who they are. In marketing, you want to stereotype. By defining who your best customers have been, you know where to look for your most likely customers. This process is called **market segmentation** or defining your **target markets**. You may wish to refer to earlier notes and use them as you complete this section.

Key Words

Small businesses that identify the needs of specific target markets—existing and potential customers who are the focus of marketing efforts—and work to satisfy those needs, are more effective marketers. Businesses identify their target markets by grouping potential users of a product or service who share similar characteristics into relatively homogeneous customer groups.

By choosing target markets, a business rejects the **mass market approach** of using the same promotional, pricing and place strategies to reach all customers. Multiple target market and concentrated target market approaches tend to be more effective for small businesses. Both approaches acknowledge that customers have different needs better served by unique product, pricing, promotion and distribution strategies.

Key Word

It is not uncommon to hear owner/managers argue that their business is too small to practice market segmentation. They insist that they must try to sell to everyone to start in business. But it is obvious what happens when you try to be everything to everyone—no one ends up happy.

Before you fall for this fallacy, consider this example. A life insurance agent, a true believer in his or her product, thinks everyone should own a policy. But there's no way an agent can reach everyone who needs insurance. How should he or she target the market?

The insurance agent could take a mass market approach, offering one product to all potential customers using the same promotional, pricing and place strategies. That approach is based on the belief that all potential life insurance customers share the same need for the same type of insurance. In that case, they should all respond to the same canned sales presentation. The mass market approach is depicted in Figure 2.1 on p. 58.

To avoid the pitfall of spreading your company's marketing too thin, smart marketers choose to subdivide the market into groups, fine tune their product or service for each group, and develop a marketing plan for each group.

FYI

Figure 2.1: Mass Market Approach

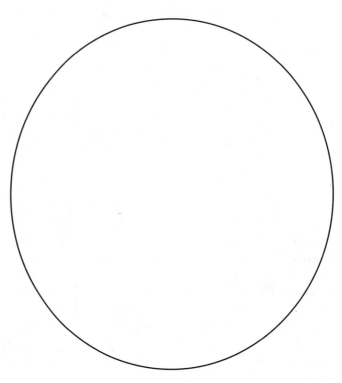

Obviously, the insurance agent needs to rethink this position. A young couple with children buys life insurance for different reasons than an older childless couple or a single man or woman. All of those prospects need different types of policies, different amounts of coverage. A mass market approach will not meet the needs of the insurance agent's customer population.

Businesses that settle for a mass market approach often end up falling behind competitors that do segment their markets and develop unique marketing plans to better meet customer needs. Unfortunately, many small business owners and managers choose mass market strategies because they see them as the cheapest and least time-consuming way to reach the widest audience. It ends up being the most expensive way, because they waste promotional dollars reaching people not likely to become customers, and have a difficult time getting the attention of potential customers.

Segmenting Your Market: Two Approaches

Key Word

The **multiple target market** approach divides a market into subgroups based on demographic, geographic, psychographic, usage rates and/or customer behaviors.

FYI

> **The Mass Market Approach**
>
> One product/service, one price, one promotion, one distribution method to reach every customer.

Figure 2.2: Multiple Target Market Approach

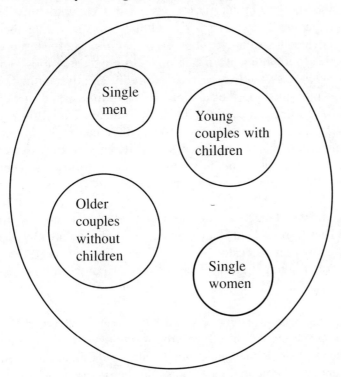

Once the market is segmented, the small business owner/manager develops different marketing strategies to reach each group. The multiple target market approach is illustrated in Figure 2.2.

It is reasonable to assume that most young couples with children share the same needs for life insurance, just as older childless couples or single men or women would. The agent can segment the market along those demographic lines and develop different products, prices and promotional strategies for each group.

The advantages of multiple target markets are that they:

• allow a personalized approach to customers

• allow you to be different things to different people

• avoid wasted promotional efforts

The potential disadvantage is that this method may be more time consuming.

A Multiple Target Market Approach   ***FYI***

Different product/service, different price, different distribution method and different promotions for each different market identified.

Profit Plus Accounting Services, Nancy Robinson: I have selected the multiple target market approach. I know that my clients' knowledge of their industries is vital to my providing them with good advice. I specialize in working with entrepreneurial companies in the food, home fashions and clothing categories. These types of businesses tend to be run by highly creative individuals who need to be constantly pushing the fashion and taste limits, and this often conflicts with the need to be sound financial managers. Basically, they come up with the product vision and I help them see if they can make money from it. Of course, once they start to produce, I also make sure they exercise tight cost controls. I accept other clients when they fall into my lap, such as food retailers, but I do not actively seek them out.

Key Word

The **concentrated target market** approach selects one or two groups as target markets. Those groups may be selected because they are the wealthiest prospects, the most regular customers or the most likely to need a new product or service. Once the target group is selected, a marketing mix strategy is devised for that group. The concentrated target market approach is shown in Figure 2.3.

Here's how the insurance agent could use the concentrated market approach. The agent divides the market into three groups: young couples with children, childless couples and single men and women with no children. The agent knows each group offers many potential customers. But he or she decides that time will be best spent calling on one group—couples with children. The agent selects this group because experience shows that this group is most likely to buy insurance. This does not mean the agent will not sell insurance to other people. It means that he or she will focus his selling and promotional efforts on one group.

Using the concentrated target market approach, small business owners and managers can really get to know and understand one aspect of the market. It is less expensive and time consuming than targeting multiple target markets. Since there is some danger in getting too selective with market efforts, this is usually a short run approach. Once the selected market is saturated, the small business owner moves to the multiple target approach by selecting another market on which to focus.

Le Caribe Wholesalers, Marie Nelson: Le Caribe selected the concentrated marketing approach. We focus our marketing efforts on selling products to ethnic foods stores. We do not actively seek out restaurants, grocery stores or other retailers who may purchase the products we sell. Once we have gained a foothold in the ethnic food store market, we will begin to focus on restaurants as well.

FYI

A Concentrated Target Group

Select the "best group." Then select the products/services, prices, distribution methods and promotions most likely to appeal to this group.

Figure 2.3: Concentrated Target Market Approach

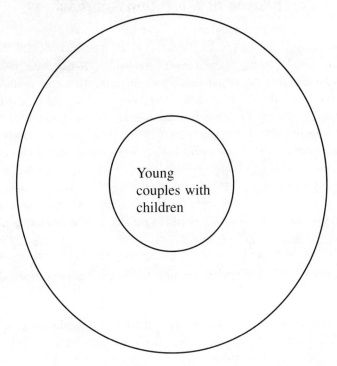

Young
couples with
children

Table 2.1 on p. 62 is an overview of the marketing approaches discussed. The major mistake that many businesses make is not sufficiently differentiating their customer bases and developing product and promotional strategies for each one.

Targeting Customers

Look for factors that will distinguish a potential customer from a not so likely customer as well as one customer group from another.

Consumer Markets

For consumer markets, these factors may include **demographics** or **psychographics**. Demographics, as listed below, addresses the physical aspect of the customer, their social status, where they live, their education, etc.

Key Words

age	income	race
sex	occupation	nationality
family size	education	social class
family life cycle	religion	location

How do you approach your product/service? Do you focus on a mass market, many target markets or one target market? Do you have the human and financial resources to focus on more than one market at a time? (A comparison of marketing approaches is shown in Table 2.1 on p. 62.)

FYI

Table 2.1: A Comparison of Marketing Approaches

Mass Market	*Multiple Target Markets*	*Concentrated Target Market*
Don't select	Select many groups	Select 'best' group
Everything for everyone	Something for everyone	"All eggs in one basket"
Expensive to reach market often enough to make an impact	Expensive to execute many marketing plans for each group	Less expensive because of focus on one market
Less time consuming to create and implement one marketing plan	More time consuming to create and implement many marketing plans	Less time consuming to create and implement one marketing plan

Psychographics deal more with the psychological influences on the customer. They are:

needs	interests
attitudes	opinions
activities	lifestyle

Target marketing is still an inexact science. Using target marketing, you may increase response to a direct mail campaign from two to three percent. But that still means that 97 percent did not respond. Target marketing helps keep you from sending your message to the wrong people.

The smaller you make the targets, the more likely you are to hit the bull's eye. You will be able to determine the hot button for each market group rather than communicating that you are all things to all people. You will be able to select the most cost efficient medium for reaching each market, and minimize the waste in your promotional strategies.

Personal Workshop Preparation #7: Consumer Markets

In completing this workshop, try to divide your customers and potential customers into the smallest groups or targets possible. Identify the key demographic/psychographic characteristics that describe each segment of your market. Under each market, write down the description of your most likely customers. Finally, make an attempt to estimate the size of each segment. You may want to describe it simply as large, medium or small.

Before you begin, you may want to observe how Jerry Lee, owner of Trade Winds Grocery, completed this workshop.

THE PURPOSE OF THIS WORKSHOP IS TO DEFINE THE DIFFERENT NICHES THAT YOU SERVE; TO BEGIN TO PRIORITIZE THE NICHES THAT YOU COULD SERVE; TO GIVE YOU AN IDEA OF HOW DIFFERENT YOUR MARKETS MAY BE.

Personal Workshop #7
Consumer Markets

	Market A	Market B	Market C
Age	25-49	25-49	25-49
Sex	Female	Female	Female
Family Life Cycle	School Age Children	No Kids	School Age Children
Income	$40,000+	$40,000+	$40,000+
Occupation	Homemaker	Professional	Professional
Education	n/a	College	College
Location	5 mile radius	5 mile radius	5 mile radius
Market Size from Census Data	900	1,200	2,000

THE PURPOSE OF THIS WORKSHOP IS TO DEFINE THE DIFFERENT NICHES THAT YOU SERVE; TO BEGIN TO PRIORITIZE THE NICHES THAT YOU COULD SERVE; TO GIVE YOU AN IDEA OF HOW DIFFERENT YOUR MARKETS MAY BE.

Personal Workshop #7
Consumer Markets

	Market A	Market B	Market C
Age			
Sex			
Family Life Cycle			
Income			
Occupation			
Education			
Location			
Market Size from Census Data			

Workshop Follow-Up

 1. Evaluate how you can segment your market into smaller groups with similar needs and wants. This will allow you to modify your product or service to better suit the needs of the small group.

 2. Develop a promotional message that speaks directly to this group.

3. Analyze how well promotional alternatives will reach each market.

Business to Business or Industrial Markets

Look for factors that will distinguish a potential customer from a not so likely customer. For business markets, these factors may include:

- standard industrial classification (SIC)
- location
- sales volume
- number of employees
- net worth
- expenditures
- dollar value added by manufacturing
- number of plants

In business to business or industrial marketing, define what companies are likely to use your product, and also define who in the company uses the product and who is involved in the purchase decision.

- decision maker
- influencer
- gatekeeper
- user

Personal Workshop Preparation #8: Business/Industrial Markets

In completing this workshop, try to divide your customers and potential customers into the smallest groups or targets possible. Identify the key characteristics that describe each segment of your market. Under each market, write down the description of your most likely customers. Finally, make an attempt to estimate the size of each segment. Your may want to describe it simply as large, medium or small.

As a preview, observe how Jim Copeland, owner of Paradise Potions, completed this workshop.

THE PURPOSE OF THIS WORKSHOP IS TO DEFINE THE DIFFERENT NICHES THAT YOU SERVE; TO BEGIN TO PRIORITIZE THE NICHES THAT YOU COULD SERVE; TO GIVE YOU AN IDEA OF HOW DIFFERENT YOUR MARKETS MAY BE.

Marketing Workshop #8
Business/Industrial Markets

	Market A	Market B	Market C
SIC	5411 Grocery	5499 Misc. stores	5812 Eating food stores places
Number of Employees	n/a	n/a	n/a
Geographic Location	6 states	6 states	6 states
Carry Ethnic Products	Yes	Yes	Yes
Part of a National Chain	No	No	Yes or No
Decision Maker	Owner	Owner	Owner
Gatekeeper	Asst. Mgr.	Asst. Mgr.	Asst. Mgr.
Size of Market from County Business Patterns	11,220	600	36,540

THE PURPOSE OF THIS WORKSHOP IS TO DEFINE THE DIFFERENT NICHES THAT YOU SERVE; TO BEGIN TO PRIORITIZE THE NICHES THAT YOU COULD SERVE; TO GIVE YOU AN IDEA OF HOW DIFFERENT YOUR MARKETS MAY BE.

Marketing Workshop #8
Business/Industrial Markets

	Market A	Market B	Market C
SIC			
Number of Employees			
Geographic Location			
Carry Ethnic Products			
Part of a National Chain			
Decision Maker			
Gatekeeper			
Size of Market from County Business Patterns			

Workshop Follow-Up

 1. Evaluate how you can segment your market into smaller groups with similar needs and wants. This will allow you to modify your product or service to better suit the needs of the small group.

 2. Develop a promotional message that speaks directly to this group.

3. Analyze how well promotional alternatives will reach each market.

Customers' Needs

Now that you have defined your specific markets, take a look at what and why customers buy. As you answer these questions from your customer's point of view, you may uncover modifications to your product or service that will better fill the needs of a specific market. This information will be valuable in developing your promotional message, so if you don't know the answer, ask your customers or potential customers.

Personal Workshop Preparation #9: Understanding My Customers' Needs

What does Jerry Lee, owner of Trade Winds Grocery, think his customers need and want? Observe how he completed the next workshop.

Personal Notes

_____

_____

_____

_____

THE PURPOSE OF THIS WORKSHOP IS TO GAIN AN UNDERSTANDING OF HOW DIFFERENT NICHES DIFFER; TO DETERMINE WHAT IS MOST IMPORTANT TO EACH MARKET SEGMENT; TO PROVIDE IDEAS FOR PRODUCT OR SERVICE IMPROVEMENTS; TO PROVIDE IDEAS FOR PROMOTIONAL MESSAGES.

Personal Workshop #9
Understanding My Customers' Needs

	Market A	Market B	Market C
How do your customers perceive your products/services?	High quality	Unique	Convenient
What do they want from a business like yours?	High quality, nutritious ideas for meals	Out of the ordinary; can be cooked for 1 or 2 and for large groups	Different and can be cooked quickly and easily
What goods or services should you be marketing?	High quality ethnic foods	Sensational foods from Asia, South America and the Caribbean	Ethnic foods that are convenient to prepare
What can you do to make it easy for people to buy from you?	Have convenient parking, have taste testings in store	Be open until at least 7 P.M., have taste testing in store	Be open until at least 7 P.M., have taste testings, deliver

THE PURPOSE OF THIS WORKSHOP IS TO GAIN AN UNDERSTANDING OF HOW DIFFERENT NICHES DIFFER; TO DETERMINE WHAT IS MOST IMPORTANT TO EACH MARKET SEGMENT; TO PROVIDE IDEAS FOR PRODUCT OR SERVICE IMPROVEMENTS; TO PROVIDE IDEAS FOR PROMOTIONAL MESSAGES.

Personal Workshop #9
Understanding My Customers' Needs

	Market A	Market B	Market C
How do your customers perceive your products/services?			
What do they want from a business like yours?			
What goods or services should you be marketing?			
What can you do to make it easy for people to buy from you?			

Workshop Follow-Up

 1. Determine what your market niches want.

 2. Modify your product or service to better meet their needs.

 3. Develop a promotional message that will motivate your market niches to purchase your product or service.

Estimating Market Demand for Your Product/Service

Part of learning about your competitor's is identifying how much of the market they control; their share of the market. If you have information about this it can help you identify opportunities as well as helping to keep your competitors' actions in perspective. Do not forget that you should also use this information to determine your share of the market.

There are a variety of methods you can use to determine your market share. If you live in a larger population area you might want to go to the library and find the latest edition of *Sales & Marketing Management's Forecast of Market Potentials*. This annual tells you how much money is spent on a variety of products and services (e.g., entertainment, clothing, automobiles, etc.) in different parts of the United States. It breaks down the amount of money spent by important demographic variables (primarily age, family size, education and family size, and sex). This report can also be of great assistance if you are considering several different geographic locations and are trying to identify the market with the population composition closest to your target market.

As noted there are many different methods to identify the size of your market. Marketers often refer to the size of a market as the **market potential**. Marketers use the term "market potential" to describe the total annual sales of a product or service by all businesses providing that product or service to a specific segment of the market. Market potential can be expressed in terms of units or in dollars. For example, the market potential for photocopier paper sold to the educational market in Wisconsin during the coming year could be "X" reams or "Y" cartons or "Z" dollars.

Key Word

Why is it important to know the market potential? An estimate of the size of the market, combined with information about your competitors, will be necessary to calculate the share of the market you hold, as well as the market shares of your competitors. Market potential figures are also useful in developing sales forecasts.

Estimating Market Potential

The precise methodology you use to estimate market potential for your market(s) will vary depending on the type of business or industry you are in. Sometimes market potential figures are available from government agencies or trade associations and you may not need to make any calculations yourself. However, most of the time market potential figures will not be readily available and you will have to develop your own estimate. The general approach to market size determination requires several steps summarized below and on Personal Workshop #10.

1. Define your target market : Begin with the information you provided in Personal Workshop #7 or #8. The more detail you can provide, the better.

You also have to define your market geographically. A manufacturer may be able to serve very large geographic area markets. But the market served by a retailer or a service firm in a large city may only be a neighborhood comprised of a dozen blocks. A direct mail business may serve national or even international markets. Your geographic market also may change over time.

Complete this step by combining the customer description with the geographic definition to arrive at the number of prospective customers in the market. For example, if you define your market as all female heads of households with annual incomes of $25,000 to $40,000 in Eau Claire and Chippewa counties, a trip to the library will give you the number you are looking for.

2. Determine the rate of consumption or usage: You need to find out or estimate the rate of consumption by users of your product or service. The rate of consumption should be expressed as an annual total or average. For example, if you have an ice cream store, you have to find out or estimate the amount of ice cream a "typical" customer will buy each year. If you provide carpet cleaning services for commercial customers, how often does a "typical" customer need this service?

3. Calculate the potential annual purchases in your target market: This is simply the result of step 1 multiplied by the result of step 2.

4. Estimate your sales volume: Multiply the market potential (from step 3) by the percent of the business you are aiming to capture, to estimate your potential volume.

5. Determine your ceiling price: You need to decide or estimate how much a customer will pay for each unit of product or service sold. In the next Challenge, you will investigate how to set the price for your product.

6. Project your dollar volume: Multiply your estimate sales volume in Step 4 by your selling price in Step 5. This figure is an estimate of the dollar volume you will generate from that specific market.

Determining the size of your market probably is not something that you will be able to do while sitting in your office or at home. One of the best sources of information may be a major public or university library. Contact the reference section to see if they carry census data on the consumers you are targeting. If you are targeting businesses, the publication *County Business Patterns* (Gordon

FYI

Another source of information to determine the size of your target market is mail list brokers (see mailing lists in the yellow pages). Call a mail list broker, and ask for some suggestions on how mailing lists can be used to help you reach the market you describe. Use the counts you obtain as a conservative estimate of the size of the market.

Table 2.2: Sources of Industry/Trade Data

Type of Business	*Possible Sources of Consumption Information*
Consumer Products—Retail Consumer Services	MediaMark Research (Research Co.) Simmons (Research Co.) *Consumer Expenditure Survey* (BLS) (Gordon Press) Trade associations
Consumer Products—Wholesaling	Census of Retail Trade (Pub. by U.S. government) Trade associations MediaMark Research (Research Co.) Simmons (Research Co.) *Consumer Expenditure Survey* (BLS) (Gordon Press)
Industrial Products—Manufacturing, Wholesaling	Census of Manufacturers Trade associations

Press, 1995) will be helpful to you. The "Annual Buyer's Guide" issue of *Sales & Marketing Management* (New York: Bill Communications), is an excellent source of information about sales of products broken down by county.

There are many good "secondary data" sources in the library. For example, *The Buying Power Survey* (Rector Press, 1994) provides detailed demographic and retail sales statistics for every county in the United States. Trade publications and trade associations are also excellent sources of information you will need. For example, the National Tire Dealers' Association does its own surveys on the demographic characteristics of tire buyers, how much people spend on tires and how often they buy them.

A brief summary of some sources that may be helpful to you are listed in Table 2.2.

To determine your market size you may have to be somewhat creative. You will have to answer questions about the characteristics of your customers and then search for information about them. For example, if you sell a fishing-related product to the general public, you will want to find information about the people in your selected geographic area who participate in that sport. Perhaps that information will be available through a state agency that sells fishing licenses. If you provide a service to female homeowners who have incomes in excess of $40,000 per year, you could look to census data to find out how many women fit that category in your selected geographic area. If you market a food product to a particular ethnic group, information about that group will typically be available from census data.

Personal Workshop Preparation #10: Estimating My Dollar Volume

Use the next Personal Workshop to estimate the dollar volume you can expect from a particular target market. This may help you to prioritize your efforts toward each market you choose to target.

Before you begin the next Personal Workshop #10, follow the example given for Paradise Potions.

THE PURPOSE OF THIS WORKSHOP IS TO QUALIFY THE SIZE OF EACH MARKET NICHE; TO ESTIMATE THE POTENTIAL OF EACH ARKET NICHE; TO PROVIDE A POTENTIAL FUNDER WITH OBJECTIVE PROOF THAT YOU HAVE A VIABLE BUSINESS IDEA; TO DETERMINE WHETHER YOU CAN GENERATE THE REVENUE THAT YOU NEED TO BE SUCCESSFUL IN BUSINESS.

Personal Workshop #10
Estimating My Dollar Volume

Steps in Determining Demand Estimation	Demand for Your Product or Service Paradise Potions
1. Define your target market	1. Ethnic food stores in the U.S. • 1524 ethnic food stores on D&B mailing list
2. Define the rate of consumption or usage	2. Estimate the average purchase per year per customer • from past customer records • 20 jars per month = 240 jars per year
3. Calculate the potential annual purchases in your target market (Multiply Step 1 times Step 2)	3. Potential purchases per year • 1524 stores x 240 jars = 365,760 jars
4. Estimate your sales volume	4. Estimate of my total volume • 5% in first year • 5% of 365,760 jars = 18,288 jars
5. Determine your selling price	5. My selling price • $1.25 per jar (wholesale)
6. Project your dollar volume (Take the result of Step 4 x Step 5)	6. Projected sales in dollars • 18,288 jars x $1.25 = $22,860

THE PURPOSE OF THIS WORKSHOP IS TO QUALIFY THE SIZE OF EACH MARKET NICHE; TO ESTIMATE THE POTENTIAL OF EACH MARKET NICHE; TO PROVIDE A POTENTIAL FUNDER WITH OBJECTIVE PROOF THAT YOU HAVE A VIABLE BUSINESS IDEA; TO DETERMINE WHETHER YOU CAN GENERATE THE REVENUE THAT YOU NEED TO BE SUCCESSFUL IN BUSINESS.

Personal Workshop #10
Estimating My Dollar Volume

Steps in Determining Demand Estimation	*Demand for Your Product or Service*
1. Define your target market	
2. Define the rate of consumption or usage	
3. Calculate the potential annual purchases in your target market (Multiply Step 1 times Step 2)	
4. Estimate your sales volume	
5. Determine your selling price	
6. Project your dollar volume (Take the result of Step 4 x Step 5)	

Workshop Follow-Up

 1. Decide if you have a feasible business idea.

2. Determine what your expenses will be and subtract them from the expected revenue to project net income.

Assessing Your Competition

As important as focusing on the customer is, a firm also must base its strategies on its strengths in view of its competitors' strengths and weaknesses. It makes little sense to go square up against a more formidable opponent. If a small firm is facing off against a stronger competitor, it should avoid imitating the competition's strategy and tactics.

Key Word

Understanding your competitors' strategies helps to anticipate their next moves and their reactions to your strategic and tactical moves. You can learn from your competitors and strengthen your business. You can predict their plans if you observe them closely. To be successful in today's economy, you need to find a **competitive edge**. Your competitive edge is the way that you satisfy your customer's needs better than your competitors do.

Assessing your competition helps focus your attention on your competitors. Recall from the first section of this book how you described your competition and how to find more information about your competitors. Remember that part of the manager's job is to identify future obstacles that come between where you are today and where you want to be in the future. This is where competitor intelligence is critical. You don't have to be a spy, but you always should be observant.

"It does not do to leave a dragon out of your calculations, if you live near him."

—J. R. Tolkien

Who is your competition? When you begin the next Personal Workshop, you may find it easier to start with a limited number of competitors, probably your biggest. Depending upon your situation, you may need to add cells for additional competitors. Don't forget your indirect competition. For example, if you are in the restaurant business, include your major competitors but don't overlook take home services or delicatessens from grocery stores.

What are your competitors' strengths? Answer this question from your point of view, the point of view of your employees, the point of view of your sales force, and the point of view of your customers. It may be helpful to solicit your customers' opinions to help identify these features. Be sure to include information that you know to be true and perceptions that the target market has of each business. This might include a variety of items; it could be their knowledgeable sales force, a great service department, their supply of parts, a responsive delivery system, a convenient location, the reputation or images that people have of the business, or their financial resources. You may find one of these traits to also be one of their weaknesses. Can you describe the direction their growth has taken? What portion of the market have they captured? Are they likely to be a future competitor?

To collect information on your competition, use the file folder method. Rather than filing all the tidbits of information you receive in your brain, take a moment to write them down and drop them in a file folder. Within six months, you will have a fairly complete competitive analysis.

Below are a number of factors for which you may want to collect information on your competition. To eliminate paralysis by analysis, look at each factor and ask if having that information would be helpful in making a marketing decision. If not, don't bother collecting the information. For the factors that are important, find information piece by piece using the competition's advertising, press releases, promotional material, your observations, comments from vendors, customers, employees, friends and business advisors. If you keep a file folder for each competitor, you can collect the following information during your everyday activities and retrieve the information when you are ready to plan.

Product/service(s)
Number of employees
Financial strength
Pricing strategy
Geographic sales territory
Positioning
Product weaknesses
Quality image
Guarantees
Personal selling strategies
Media used and expenditures
Customer service policy
Employees' sales ability
Distribution advantage
Appearance and design of store
How they compete with you
Their weaknesses

Years in business
Dollar sales (current, growth/decline)
Profitability
Target market
Marketing objectives
Product strengths
Added services
Reliability
Promotion strategies
Advertising themes
Publicity/public relations efforts
Employees' product knowledge
Availability of products
Convenience of locations
Merchandising strategy
Their strengths

Personal Workshop Preparation #11: Assessing My Competition

Write out the types of information that you would like to gather about your competition. Then fill in the information that you have. Pass it around to your employees to fill in information they have. Check the yellow pages, or other places where your competitors may advertise. Then go to the reference section of the library to see what other information is available.

You may first want to examine how Nancy Robinson, owner of Profit Plus Accounting Services, completed this exercise.

To gather information about your competition, ask your customers. Whenever you don't get the sale, take off your selling hat and put on your market research hat. Explain to the customer that you are very interested in improving your product/service/business. Then ask what the competition has that you do not have.

FYI

PROFIT PLUS
ACCOUNTING SERVICE
NANCY ROBINSON

THE PURPOSE OF THIS WORKSHOP IS TO GAIN AN UNDERSTANDING OF YOUR COMPETITORS' STRENGTHS AND WEAKNESSES; TO PROVIDE A FRAMEWORK TO MEASURE YOUR BUSINESS AGAINST YOUR COMPETITION; TO PROVIDE INSIGHT INTO THE MOST LUCRATIVE STRATEGIES FOR YOUR BUSINESS; TO PROVIDE INFORMATION NEEDED TO DIFFERENTIATE YOURSELF FROM YOUR COMPETITION.

Personal Workshop #11
Assessing My Competition

	Competitor A	Competitor B
Years in Business	20 years	2 years
Number of Employees	2	0
Target Market	Businesses with 10+ employees	Anyone
Positioning	We have experience	We are inexpensive
Strengths	Strong in tax	Inexpensive
Weaknesses	Lack knowledge of bookkeeping software	No real expertise
Technical Abilities	Strong in tax; don't do audits; okay for reviews and compilations	Mediocre in all areas
Customer Service	Needs work	They try

FYI

To gather information about your competitors, ask your suppliers. But remember your suppliers will be willing to share information on your company with your competitors as well.

THE PURPOSE OF THIS WORKSHOP IS TO GAIN AN UNDERSTANDING OF YOUR COMPETITORS' STRENGTHS AND WEAKNESSES; TO PROVIDE A FRAMEWORK TO MEASURE YOUR BUSINESS AGAINST YOUR COMPETITION; TO PROVIDE INSIGHT INTO THE MOST LUCRATIVE STRATEGIES FOR YOUR BUSINESS; TO PROVIDE INFORMATION NEEDED TO DIFFERENTIATE YOURSELF FROM YOUR COMPETITION.

Personal Workshop #11
Assessing My Competition

	Competitor A	Competitor B
Years in Business		
Number of Employees		
Target Market		
Positioning		
Strengths		
Weaknesses		
Technical Abilities		
Customer Service		

Workshop Follow-Up

 1. Compile information about who your major competitors are, and what they have to offer to customers, and what their strengths and weaknesses are.

 2. Use this information to position your product or service as different and better than your competitor in ways that are important to your customer.

Looking at Your Business

The first three sections of the situation analysis required the collection and organization of a great number of pieces of information about the environment in which you operate, who your most likely customers are, what your most likely customers want, and the strengths and weaknesses of your competition. Now comes the time to look at your own business from both your point of view and that of your customers.

Identify the resources available for eventual execution of plans in terms of manpower, knowledge, skills, capital, facilities, equipment and other resources. Answer the questions:

- What have we done right?

- What have we done wrong?

- Have we done the right things?

Conducting a SWOT Analysis

One simple way to compile this information is to conduct a SWOT (strengths, weaknesses, opportunities and threats) analysis. Using the categories listed below to stimulate your thinking, hold a brainstorming session with yourself and your key employees to uncover your strengths, weaknesses, opportunities and threats. First look at them from your point of view, then try to look at

> *"There is no right way to do the wrong thing."*

them from your customers' point of view. If you can't list your strengths and weaknesses from your customers' point of view, you may want to invite your customers to a focus group to share their thoughts with you.

The only rule in brainstorming is no criticism. Every idea gets listed. No ideas get discussed. If you plan to include different levels of employees, hold separate brainstorming sessions for managers and employees.

Strengths

Points to be further enhanced	Business strengths
Quality/design/performance	Production/cost/price
Marketing effectiveness	Personnel
Financial resources	Facilities
Relationships with suppliers	

Weaknesses

Points that need to be corrected	Quality/design/performance
Production/cost/price	Marketing effectiveness
Personnel	Financial resources
Facilities	Relationships with suppliers

Opportunities

Can I change this circumstance? How long will these advantages last —and how can my business best take advantage of these circumstances?

Can I take advantage of or build on this?

Threats

If it is beyond my control, how will it affect my business?

How long will these disadvantages last —and how can my business best take advantage of these circumstances?

Personal Workshop Preparation #12: SWOT Analysis

Meet with your employees to brainstorm your strengths, weaknesses, opportunities and threats. Be sure to list every one given, whether you agree with it or not. You can evaluate and prioritize later.

Marie Nelson held a brainstorming session with her employees at Le Caribe Wholesalers. The next Personal Workshop reveals her findings.

> *"Successful people have formed the habit of doing the things that failures don't like to do."*
>
> —Albert E. N. Gray

THE PURPOSE OF THIS WORKSHOP IS TO UNCOVER YOUR STRENGTHS AND WEAKNESSES; TO LOOK AT YOUR BUSINESS FROM YOUR CUSTOMERS' POINT OF VIEW; TO DISCOVER POTENTIAL OPPORTUNITIES OR THREATS.

Personal Workshop #12
SWOT Analysis

Strengths	*Weaknesses*
Good relationship with retailers	I don't delegate enough
Stays on top of food trends	The business is not computerized
A good understanding of the operations of the business	Knowledge of retailers' needs is lost

Opportunities	*Threats*
Good chance to get into a national chain	One of the partners is near retirement and may be bought out
Could add Asian food products to the product line	

THE PURPOSE OF THIS WORKSHOP IS TO UNCOVER YOUR STRENGTHS AND WEAKNESSES; TO LOOK AT YOUR BUSINESS FROM YOUR CUSTOMERS' POINT OF VIEW; TO DISCOVER POTENTIAL OPPORTUNITIES OR THREATS.

Personal Workshop #12
SWOT Analysis

Strengths   *Weaknesses*

Opportunities   *Threats*

Workshop Follow-Up

 1. Look at your business from your point of view, from your employees' point of view and most importantly from your customers' point of view.

 2. Use this information to assure that you build on your strengths and minimize your weaknesses as you plan your marketing strategies.

Company Image

Image is one of a company's most essential assets. That image exists in the minds of customers the company wants to attract. It can be positive, negative or non-existent. A non-existent image is almost as bad as a negative one.

What product or service establishment do customers think of when they want to buy? Where do they go first to shop? If your business is not one of the first stops customers consider, you don't have a good image. The companies on the top of consumers' shopping lists are the market leaders. These companies enjoy "top-of-the-mind awareness."

> *"Small opportunities are often the beginning of great enterprises."*
> —Demosthenes

Owners and managers need to examine objectively how other people view them, their business and their products and/or services. On a regular basis, those inside the business should take a close look at sales staff, customer contacts, phone service, hours of operation, products and services, building and parking, and billing. Then they should ask their customers about those same issues.

Once business owners/managers have compared their perspectives to that of their customers, the next step is determining how to improve that image. A company's image is made up of:

- Selection of products and/or services

- Communication with the target market

- Prices of products and/or services

- Appearance of business, inside and out

- Company policies

- Customer conveniences, including location, hours of operation and parking

- Customer service

Personal Workshop Preparation #13: A Look at My Business

Answer the following questions as honestly as you can about your business. You may want to ask your employees to anonymously answer the more subjective questions. If in doing this exercise you do not find anything negative about your business, go back and review your business again. If you do not find any faults or weaknesses in your business, you will not have the opportunity to correct them.

Take a look at how Jerry Lee, from Trade Winds Grocery, completed the next workshop.

THE PURPOSE OF THIS WORKSHOP IS TO LOOK AT YOUR BUSINESS FROM YOUR CUSTOMER'S POINT OF VIEW; TO DETERMINE NECESSARY CHANGES IN POLICIES OR PROCEDURES IN ORDER TO BETTER SERVE YOUR CUSTOMERS; TO DIFFERENTIATE YOURSELF FROM YOUR COMPETITION.

Personal Workshop #13
A Look At My Business

1. What are your hours of operation? (include days of week and times of day)

Sunday-Friday 11 A.M. until 7 P.M., Saturday from 10 A.M. until 6 P.M.

2. What extra services do you provide? (special orders, parking, delivery, etc.)

Offer taste tests, free parking. Special order hard to find food products.

3. What changes have you made in your business over the last two years? How have these changes impacted your business?

Added a new product line, Paradise Potions, resulting in a monthly sales volume of $4,000 per month.

4. Has your customer base changed over the last two years? If so, how?

I have not kept track of customers , so I'm not sure whether the customer base has changed.

5. How important is location for your customers? How convenient is your location for your customers?

Location is very important for customers. Being located within three blocks of a major supermarket makes it easy for customers to purchase their specialty items on their way to or from the grocery store.

6. Describe the appearance of your business, inside and out.

The sign on the outside of the business is beginning to fade. A number of different signs, some out of date, are in the window. The parking lot and sidewalk is kept clean. Inside, the store is very crowded. With the additional product lines carried, shelf space is at a premium. The shelves are neatly stocked and kept clean. The layout does encourage customers to walk throughout the store.

7. What is your customer service policy?

The customer service policy is to take care of customers. This includes letting customers taste a product before buying, providing customers with cooking tips, and providing a money back guarantee on the products sold at the taste tests.

8. From your customers' point of view, what might be a disincentive to buying from your business? (price, location, parking, selection, turnaround, etc.)

Some of the products can be found at a larger supermarket at a slightly lower price.

9. If your customers had to describe your company to a colleague in one or two sentences, what would you want them to say?

"The place to go when you want an unusual taste treat."

10. How do you promote your business?

Ads in the Thursday newspaper.

11. What do customers like about your business and its operations?

They like the assistance they receive, whether they are planning a meal or a party.

12. What would your customers change about your business and its operations if they could?

Customers would like a little more room inside the store. They would like the store to stay open until 11 PM.

13. How do your customers view your employees? Would they hire them?

Customers view my employees as knowledgeable and helpful. They would consider hiring them because they are self-motivated hard workers.

14. Why do your customers buy from you and not from your competition?

Because they can get more unusual items, and much better service.

THE PURPOSE OF THIS WORKSHOP IS TO LOOK AT YOUR BUSINESS FROM YOUR CUSTOMERS' POINT OF VIEW; TO DETERMINE NECESSARY CHANGES IN POLICIES OR PROCEDURES IN ORDER TO BETTER SERVE YOUR CUSTOMERS; TO DIFFERENTIATE YOURSELF FROM YOUR COMPETITION.

Personal Workshop #13
A Look At My Business

1. What are your hours of operation? (include days of week and times of day)

2. What extra services do you provide? (special orders, parking, delivery, etc.)

3. What changes have you made in your business over the last two years? How have these changes impacted your business?

4. Has your customer base changed over the last two years? If so, how?

5. How important is location for your customers? How convenient is your location for your customers?

6. Describe the appearance of your business, inside and out.

7. What is your customer service policy?

8. From your customers' point of view, what might be a disincentive to buying from your business? (price, location, parking, selection, turnaround, etc.)

9. If your customers had to describe your company to a colleague in one or two sentences, what would you want them to say?

10. How do you promote your business?

11. What do your customers like about your business and its operations?

12. What would your customers change about your business and its operations if they could?

13. How do your customers view your employees? Would they hire them?

14. Why do your customers buy from you and not from your competition?

Workshop Follow-Up

1. Take a look at your business from your customers' eyes. This will help uncover modifications that need to be made in your product or service, in your customer service system, in the way you get your product or service to your customers, and in your overall operations.

2. Use this information to improve your quality and service level in the eyes of your customers, and to develop a promotional message that will motivate prospects to buy from you.

Make a Comparison

Now that you have taken a close look at your competition and at your business, you need to compare your business to your competitors. You will want to focus on the areas of business that have the greatest impact on your success. As you compare yourself to your competition remember to look at each business from the eyes of your customers. Remember, each of your market niches may see things differently. For that reason, you will want to complete the following workshop for each of the niches you will target.

Personal Workshop Preparation #14: Critical Success Factors

1. Identify Critical Success Factors: Start out by thinking about what factors are critical to the success of a business like yours.

For example, if you had a restaurant you would want to make a list of the factors that customers consider in deciding to eat at your place. These might include factors such as:

- Appealing Food
- Affordable Prices
- Cleanliness
- Selection of Items
- Smoking/Non-smoking Sections

- Pleasant Atmosphere
- Convenient Location
- Friendly Service
- Family Sections
- Healthy Entrees

Fill in the factors that are critical for a business such as yours to be successful. Put your factors in column A.

2. Weigh each Success Factor by Importance: Some of the factors are probably more important than others. Take 100 points and divide them among the factors you identified to reflect the relative importance of each factor. Place your weights in column B.

Hint: It may help to start out assigning a weight to the most important factor. Then weigh the least important factor. Now, weigh the most important of those factors remaining, followed by the least important, until you have assigned all 100 points to your factors.

3. Rate your Business: For each success factor, rate the performance of your business using a scale of 1 (low) to 10 (high). Put your business' rating in column C. Add all the points in the column and write down the total.

4. Calculate your Scores: Multiple your critical Success Factor Weights times your Ratings (B x C). Place your result in the next column labeled Score.

5. Evaluate your Competitors: Using the procedures outline in Steps 3 and 4, rate your competitors on each critical success factor and calculate their scores.

6. Calculate the Overall Scores for each Business: Total the number of points for each business in the bottom row to determine the overall score for the businesses you included.

As a preview of the next workshop, examine how Jim Copeland of Paradise Potions, completed this exercise for the restaurant market.

Personal Notes

_____

_____

_____

_____

THE PURPOSE OF THIS WORKSHOP IS TO IDENTIFY THE FACTORS CRITICAL TO THE SUCCESS OF YOUR BUSINESS; TO PRIORITIZE THE IMPORTANCE OF EACH OF THESE FACTORS; TO RATE YOUR BUSINESS AND YOUR COMPETITORS ON EACH OF THESE FACTORS; TO DETERMINE WHAT YOU NEED TO CHANGE TO BRING YOUR BUSINESS UP TO PAR WITH YOUR COMPETITION; TO DETERMINE WHAT FACTORS YOU CAN CAPITALIZE ON TO GAIN NEW CUSTOMERS.

Personal Workshop #14
Critical Success Factors

A. Critical Success Factors	B. Weights or Importance (out of 100)	Your Business		Competitor A		Competitor B		Competitor C	
		C. Your Ratings	Score (B x C)	D. A's Ratings	Score (B x D)	E. B's Ratings	Score (B x E)	F. C's Ratings	Score (B x F)
Unique flavors	25	9	225	7	175	7	175	4	100
Fresh	20	9	180	9	180	8	160	9	180
Affordable prices	10	7	70	8	80	9	90	7	70
Orders filled within 48 hours	15	7	105	7	105	5	75	9	135
Consistent quality	25	9	225	8	200	6	150	9	225
Preparation tips	5	9	45	5	25	3	15	5	25
Totals	100		850		765		665		735

THE PURPOSE OF THIS WORKSHOP IS TO IDENTIFY THE FACTORS CRITICAL TO THE SUCCESS OF YOUR BUSINESS; TO RIORITIZE THE IMPORTANCE OF EACH OF THESE FACTORS; TO RATE YOUR BUSINESS AND YOUR COMPETITORS ON EACH OF THESE FACTORS; TO DETERMINE WHAT YOU NEED TO CHANGE TO BRING YOUR BUSINESS UP TO PAR WITH YOUR COMPETITION; TO DETERMINE WHAT FACTORS YOU CAN CAPITALIZE ON TO GAIN NEW CUSTOMERS.

Personal Workshop #14
Critical Success Factors

A. Critical Success Factors	B. Weights or Importance (out of 100)	Your Business		Competitor A		Competitor B		Competitor C	
		C. Your Ratings	Score (B x C)	D. A's Ratings	Score (B x D)	E. B's Ratings	Score (B x E)	F. C's Ratings	Score (B x F)

Workshop Follow-Up

1. The resulting scores reflect how your business compares with your competitors on each factor that you identified as critical to the success of a business similar to yours. The totals should indicate the relative strengths and weakness of both your business and your competitors. A word of caution: remember that your weights and ratings are subjective and if you have a tendency to be overly optimistic it may be reflected in your scores. Likewise, if you are your own harshest critic, you may have underrated yourself. Be as objective as you can in your evaluations.

2. Low scores reflect problems. Don't overlook the insights you've uncovered. Address each of your weaknesses. Remember that a problem, when resolved, may likely become an opportunity. Think positive.

 3. Use the scores as guides or indicators and not as an end in themselves. The scoring pattern should assist you in identifying areas of opportunity and threats to your survival. Opportunities and threats occur in the business environment. They are uncontrollable, but you must constantly "keep your ear to the ground" to determine what is happening around you.

 4. Now it's time to put your hard work to use in planning your future directions! On to the next section.

The Marketing Plan: Writing Marketing Objectives

Strengths and weaknesses and opportunities and threats do not tell the decision-maker what to do. Instead they identify areas that need to be incorporated into your marketing objectives and actions.

> *"For one who has no objective, nothing is relevant."*
>
> —Confucius

Objectives are goals you want to achieve. You achieve your objectives by devising strategies or plans, each backed by a series of steps. Try to focus your objectives on products and/or services and markets. By selling or creating more value to existing or new markets, you can achieve financial goals. Changes in product, pricing, distribution, and promotion can be used as strategies to achieve your objectives.

How do you write a good objective? You might want to consider the acronym **SMART** and the characteristics it stands for in your writing. Your objective should be **specific**, not vague. It should be an action that you can **measure** your progress and not a variable that you can't. Good objectives address issues that you can **act** on, not a lofty idea. Make sure it is **realistic**; unrealistic goals set you up for failure before you even begin. Lastly, the objective should include a **time** element for start dates and finish dates.

SPECIFIC

MEASURE

ACT

REALISTIC

TIME

Objectives are desirable results achieved through your efforts, statements of what is expected from pursuing a set of business activities. Objectives give direction to your marketing effort and decide where your company should go.

Recognize the opportunities that you can capitalize on. There are many markets you can choose to serve, and needs that you can fulfill. Armed with information from your situation analysis, brainstorm what the long term possibilities for your company might be. Don't be content in just extrapolating the future based on the past. Eliminate your tunnel vision and look at all that your company could achieve.

Then analyze each of your potential objectives to see how it fits in with the mission of the company, company strengths and weaknesses, company resources and other objectives. You can't do everything. So, focus on the area that you can serve most readily and profitably, and stay with that area. When you are well-entrenched and have an established, outstanding reputation in that area, you can then expand your focus.

After you have set a direction with your longer term objectives, set goals with your short-term objectives. Make sure your objectives are really goals and not strategies. For example, the objective: *"Make 50 telemarketing calls each month,"* is not really an objective. The result you want to achieve is not 50 calls each month. The goal you want to achieve is setting up 10 sales appointments or selling five units each month. Telemarketing is one of the many strategies you may choose to achieve your goal. Short-term objectives are usually stated in terms of unit or dollar sales, number of new customers, percentage of current customers retained, number of names added to mailing list, etc.

Questions to Ask About Marketing Objectives

- Can my customers actually use as much of the product/service as I predict?

- Can I realistically produce the product/service at a competitive price and in the quantity needed?

- Do I have the financial and human resources to achieve these objectives?

- What reactions can I expect from my competition and what affect will they have?

> *"People with goals succeed because they know where they're going."*
>
> —Earl Nightingale

Using the SMART Method

Specific

- Don't use broad terms such as best, biggest, smallest.

- Don't use terms that are vague, such as more or less, minimize or maximize.

If one of your objectives is to increase sales, be sure to also include a profit objective so you don't increase sales at the expense of profits.

If one of your objectives is to obtain new customers, be sure to include an objective to retain current customers so you don't pursue new customers at the expense of current customers.

FYI

Measurable

- Don't use traits or characteristics that are difficult or impossible to measure.

Actionable

- Don't set objectives that deal with factors you cannot influence.

Realistic

- Don't set objectives that can't be achieved and consequently are not given serious consideration.

Timely

- Don't forget to include start and finish dates, otherwise you can still be working on your objective even though you may not have achieved it after years of effort.

How many objectives should you set? Write only as many as you realistically can achieve. Don't set yourself up for a fall by taking on more than you can accomplish. Five to seven good objectives is a reasonable number for most managers to handle.

Table 2.3 contrasts the **SMART** objectives with those that aren't.

Table 2.3: SMART Objectives versus those that aren't

"Do Your Best" Objectives	*SMART Objectives*
We intend to increase sales during the coming year.	Achieve a 20% share of the Wisconsin market for snow shovels by the end of 1995.
Achieve as much market share as possible for our electric dust mops.	By the end of the first quarter of 1995, 10,000 customers from the target market should have test driven the XL 5000 motor scooter.
Make our products available in the top ten metro markets.	After one month of sample product distribution in the Wausau market, have 100 former Acme rubber band customers say that Primo makes the best rubber bands on the market.

Personal Workshop Preparation #15: Objective Writing

Using the next Personal Workshop, Objective Writing, identify each market segment and the objectives you have set for each.

Take a look at one of the objectives Nancy Robinson wrote for this exercise.

THE PURPOSE OF THIS WORKSHOP IS TO LEARN TO WRITE SPECIFIC MEASURABLE OBJECTIVES; TO KEEP STRATEGIES OUT OF YOUR OBJECTIVES; TO DETERMINE WHERE YOU WANT THE BUSINESS TO GO.

PROFIT PLU$
ACCOUNTING SERVICE
NANCY ROBINSON

Personal Workshop #15

Objective Writing

Target Market Segment	Objective	Is it SMART?
Professionals in the tri-county area	Obtain five new clients with an average billing of $5,000 per year	Yes

According to creativity experts, the first solution to a problem is usually not the ideal solution, although it may be satisfactory. Use brainstorming to list all the potential strategies that may help to achieve your objective. Then evaluate each strategy idea to determine which is most cost effective and most likely to work.

THE PURPOSE OF THIS WORKSHOP IS TO LEARN TO WRITE SPECIFIC MEASURABLE OBJECTIVES; TO KEEP STRATEGIES OUT OF YOUR OBJECTIVES; TO DETERMINE WHERE YOU WANT THE BUSINESS TO GO.

Personal Workshop #15
Objective Writing

Target Market Segment	Objective	Is it SMART?

Workshop Follow-Up

 1. Make each objective as **SMART** (specific, measurable, actionable, realistic and challenging) as possible. Only by doing this will you be able to track your progress (or lack of it).

 2. Consider the priorities of your objectives — which ones are most important for you to achieve? Make sure your planning and implementation efforts reflect this ordering.

The Marketing Plan:
Developing Strategies and Action Plans

How do we get where we want to go?
When do we want to arrive?
Who is responsible?
How much will it cost?

"We cannot direct the wind... But we can adjust the sails."

—Unknown

Objectives and goals are nice, but they don't get the job done by themselves. Now comes the time to determine what actions you must take to accomplish your objectives.

Strategies or plans of action must be devised to achieve your objectives. Strategies should be thought of in broad terms. How you will accomplish your goals may be done through a variety of actions. Take time to look at what you propose before you start the implementation process. If your strategy is implemented, will it help provide your business with a competitive advantage? Take a look at how this process might work using an example.

> "Opportunity is missed by most people because it is dressed in overalls and looks like work."
>
> —Thomas Edison

Imagine that after conducting the SWOT analysis, you identified that one of your strengths was retaining customers. Unfortunately, one weakness was acquiring new customers. From this you have proposed an objective which is to add and retain five new customers who purchase $XX worth of goods/services in each of the next 12 months. How will you accomplish this task? Your response to this question becomes your strategy.

They are a variety of strategies that can help achieve this goal. The next two Challenges, "Crafting An Effective Marketing Mix" and "Communicating With Your Market" will discuss the strategies that you may choose. For example, some options might include:

- Using direct mail to generate leads

- Altering pricing of certain products and services

- Modifying or adding new products or services

- Changing the distribution system

- Using telemarketing to qualify leads

> "If you do what you have always done, you'll get what you have always gotten."

Personal Workshop Preparation #16:
My Action Plan

Managers must weigh their options and make decisions. It is obvious that several steps will be needed to implement whichever strategy you selected. Tracking all of the tasks involved in executing your plan is an important job. Many details need to be recorded and monitored. Personal Workshop #16 can be used to assist you with this task. For each objective the specific steps should be outlined. The person(s) responsible for accomplishing the task should be identified. Start and completion dates should be agreed upon. Budgets must be established to accomplish the activities.

For each objective you will have at least one strategy. Make copies of this sheet for each strategy that you will implement. Then list all of the steps necessary to implement that strategy. Start with the last step and work backwards, assigning a person responsible, and a start and finish date. Where appropriate, include the cost for that specific step.

As a preview of the next workshop, observe how Nancy Robinson completed the form for her business, Profit Plus Accounting Services.

THE PURPOSE OF THIS WORKSHOP IS TO SET OBJECTIVES AND CHOOSE STRATEGIES WHICH WILL BRING ABOUT RESULTS; TO CREATE A HABIT OF ASSIGNING AND SETTING DEADLINES FOR EACH TASK; TO THINK THROUGH WHAT IT WILL TAKE TO IMPLEMENT A STRATEGY.

Personal Workshop #16
My Action Plan

Objective: Obtain five new clients with an average billing of $5000 per year.

Strategy: Conduct presentations on managing cash flow for chambers of commerce and other professional association.

Activities to Carry Out Strategy	Person(s) Responsible	Start Date	Finish Date
Follow up with participants	Nancy Robinson	1 wk. post presentation	ongoing
Do presentation	Nancy Robinson	Presentation date	
Copy handout materials	Secretary	1 wk. prior	1 day prior
Get count from chamber or association	Secretary	1 wk. prior	1 wk. prior
Prepare handout materials	Nancy Robinson	1 mo. prior	1 wk. prior
Prepare overhead or slides	Nancy Robinson	1 wk. prior	1 day prior
Send announcement to clients and potential clients	Secretary	4 wks. prior	2 wks. prior
Develop promotional copy for chamber or association	Nancy Robinson	10 wks. prior	8 wks. prior
Schedule date with chamber or association	Nancy Robinson	10 wks. prior	
Follow up calls to chamber or associations	Nancy Robinson	1 week after scheduled date	2 weeks after scheduled date
Write promotional letter	Nancy Robinson	1 week after scheduled date	2 weeks after scheduled date

THE PURPOSE OF THIS WORKSHOP IS TO SET OBJECTIVES AND CHOOSE STRATEGIES WHICH WILL BRING ABOUT RESULTS; TO CREATE A HABIT OF ASSIGNING AND SETTING DEADLINES FOR EACH TASK; TO THINK THROUGH WHAT IT WILL TAKE TO IMPLEMENT A STRATEGY.

Personal Workshop #16
My Action Plan

Objective:

Strategy:

Activities to Carry Out Strategy	Person(s) Responsible	Start Date	Finish Date

> "The best game plan in the world never blocked or tackled anybody."
>
> —Vince Lombardi

Workshop Follow-Up

 1. By developing action plans, you will assure that you are focusing your efforts on the strategies that are important to the success of your business.

 2. By adding deadlines, you will eliminate many of the "fires" you had to put out in the past by scheduling all of the steps for a strategy. These action plans can be used to communicate to employees what is expected of them and when. It will show employees where they fit into the big picture. Action plans can be used to manage employee performance.

 3. By adding budget numbers to the steps in the plan, you can also create a projected cash flow statement.

 4. Five factors can have an enormous impact on the implementation of whatever strategy is selected:

> *"Every act of creation is first of all an act of destruction."*
>
> —Picasso

1. Consistency
2. Striving for win-win situations
3. Test marketing your ideas
4. Creating an entrepreneurial atmosphere
5. Monitoring the changing environment

Evaluate the Results

How are we doing?
Did we do what we said we would do?

Compare actual progress with planned results; investigate reasons for deviations. Initiate corrective measures; change objectives, strategies, and/or action plans or programs.

After activities are started, managers need to monitor the results of the actions and adjust or modify plans accordingly. If your objective included all the SMART characteristics, it should not be too difficult to monitor. Planning in advance how to monitor your performance may save you from trouble later. The next Personal Workshop, Monitoring My Objectives, can be used to summarize all your objectives.

Personal Workshop Preparation #17: Monitoring My Objectives

List each of your objectives. Then explain how you will monitor the progress towards each objective. Each month, add the results to the results column.

Nancy Robinson, owner of Profit Plus Accounting Services, used the next workshop to monitor the objective that she had set.

THE PURPOSE OF THIS WORKSHOP IS TO DETERMINE HOW YOU WILL MONITOR YOUR PROGRESS FOR EACH OBJECTIVE; TO PLAN TO EVALUATE WHAT IS WORKING AND WHAT IS NOT WORKING; TO PROVIDE INFORMATION TO HELP FINE TUNE YOUR PLAN.

PROFIT PLUS
ACCOUNTING SERVICE
NANCY ROBINSON

Personal Workshop #17
Monitoring My Objectives

List each of your objectives. Then explain how you will monitor the progress towards each objective. Each month, add the results to the results column.

Objective	*How Monitored*	*Results*
Obtain 5 new clients averaging $5,000 per year in billings.	Monthly count of new clients.	As of June 30, 2 new clients signed.
	Monthly review of prospective clients that are being nurtured.	As of June 30, communicating with 3 potential clients, one of whom was likely to sign.

THE PURPOSE OF THIS WORKSHOP IS TO DETERMINE HOW YOU WILL MONITOR YOUR PROGRESS FOR EACH OBJECTIVE; TO PLAN TO EVALUATE WHAT IS WORKING AND WHAT IS NOT WORKING; TO PROVIDE INFORMATION TO HELP FINE TUNE YOUR PLAN.

Personal Workshop #17
Monitoring My Objectives

List each of your objectives. Then explain how you will monitor the progress towards each objective. Each month, add the results to the results column.

Objective	*How Monitored*	*Results*

Workshop Follow-Up

 1. Determine if you are on the track toward achieving your goals. Monitoring your progress will encourage you to analyze what is working and what is not working.

 2. You should cut back on your expenses if it looks like you will not achieve your revenue goals.

You Have Completed Challenge 2

As you arrive at the end of this Challenge, you should have a solid foundation for your marketing plan. You have a better understanding of the environment in which you operate, a clear definition of your most likely customer groups, and a better understanding of the needs of your most likely customers. Keeping this information in mind, you have evaluated your business against your competition to determine why customers will buy from you instead of the competition. You have also uncovered some weaknesses in your business that need to be corrected. Based on the information you compiled, you set SMART objectives to head your business where you would like it to go. And finally, you have learned to cure insanity (doing the same thing over and over and expecting different results), by monitoring your progress; quit doing what does not work, and do more of what does work.

> "We cannot solve today's problems with the same level of thinking that created them."
>
> —Albert Einstein

In the next two Challenges, you will investigate the different marketing strategies that you may want to consider for your business. Once you have selected your strategies, you can return to this Challenge and complete an action plan for each strategy to be implemented.

You Leave Challenge 2 with the Following

 Information: You know how to complete a marketing plan. You have gained knowledge on how environmental factors will impact your business, who your most likely customers are and what they want, what your competitors strengths and weaknesses are, how your customers view your

 FYI

Questions you must ask yourself on a regular basis:

1. What are we trying to do?

2. Why is it important for us to do it?

3. How are we going to get it done?

4. How can we do it better or faster and still get good results?

5. What is the best thing we can do now in order to improve our profits?

6. Who should be doing what now to satisfy our customers' needs and to achieve our goals?

business, how to write SMART objectives, how to develop action plans, and how to monitor your results.

Tools: Each of the workshops you completed can be used as a tool to gather the information you need to plan for the success of your business and to make better business decisions.

Learning: You have learned how to use the knowledge you have gained to develop a marketing plan. By completing this process, you have a better understanding of your business, your competition, and your customers.

Networking: You have uncovered resources to obtain the information you need to make better decisions for your business. You have discovered that on a daily basis you are running across information you need to make decisions, and that by filing that information, you have access to it when you need it.

Challenge 2 Self-Assessment

After completing this Challenge you should be able to begin developing a marketing plan for your business. You will need to complete the last two Challenges to discover all the potential strategies that you may want to incorporate into your marketing plan. To check your understanding and guide you in developing your marketing plan, complete the following checklist.

Situation Analysis

( ) I can identify how the economy will impact my business over the next year.

( ) I am aware of the laws with which I must comply.

( ) I am aware of the trends which may impact the demand for my product or service.

( ) I am knowledgeable of the new technologies which affect my business.

( ) I can describe two or three niche markets that I would like to serve.

( ) I can describe what each niche wants from a business like mine.

( ) I can estimate the revenue that I can expect from each market.

( ) I can list the strengths and weaknesses of my major competitors.

**Pages
47 - 89**

**Pages
89-99**

( ) I can identify my strengths and weaknesses.

( ) I can describe my company's image from the point of view of each niche I plan to serve.

( ) I can write three to five SMART objectives.

( ) I can determine how I will measure progress towards meeting each objective.

Take Another Look

Review the results of your Challenge 2 Self-Assessment. Which areas do you still need to work on? Follow up on these areas by reviewing appropriate sections of the Challenge.

Challenge 3

Crafting An Effective Marketing Mix

A family recipe for cookies requires a special blend of ingredients, in just the right proportions, carefully combined and baked for just the right amount of time.

Similarly, to achieve a pleasing result with your company's marketing, you must carefully select your marketing activities, combining them with a keen eye toward how they interrelate and what financial resources they require. You must then blend them together to create an outcome more powerful than any one activity, and then exercise enough patience to allow them time to "bake"—to attract customer attention, generate interest and to start to create a desire to buy from your company.

This challenge is designed to provide you with a framework for evaluating the effectiveness of your current marketing strategy by examining the three key areas of marketing which combine to create your marketing mix: product development, place decisions and pricing. The marketing mix is the set of product, pricing, and place decisions made to appeal to your target market(s).

Key Ingredients

The specific decisions to be reviewed are:

- **Product/service decisions**
  product assortment
  new product development
  warranties
  branding strategies
  packaging
  labeling
  product life cycle

- **Place decisions**
  market exposure
  channels of distribution
  location
  days and hours of operation

- **Pricing decisions**
  price setting
  pricing strategy and business image
  pricing strategies and the product life cycle

The best mix of these activities varies from business to business. How you blend these elements depends on such factors as your company's objectives, its image in the marketplace, and its ability to devote economic and employee resources to marketing.

The marketing mix is also shaped by circumstances outside of your control, including:

- Demographic and cultural trends that affect the needs, habits and lifestyles of customers;

- The number of competitors and their degree of competitiveness;

- Existing and projected economic conditions;

- Technological changes; and

- Local, state, federal and/or agency laws and regulations.

Business owners and managers need to know how these factors will affect their ability to market their products and services. Some influences offer growth opportunities for a business, while others may threaten its existence.

> *"So long as new ideas are created, sales will continue to reach new highs."*
>
> —Charles Kettering

You have previously examined how you conduct your company's marketing currently, have explored the usefulness of various types of marketing research to provide needed knowledge, and have reviewed the techniques used to assemble a results-oriented marketing plan. Challenge 3 leads you into the realm of marketing strategy implementation—making your plan work to produce sales.

Part One of this Challenge presents the key decisions to be made in effective product or service development. Upon completion of Part One you will be able to:

- evaluate your product assortment from the point of view of customer satisfaction

- develop a reliable system for new product development

FYI To keep track of trends that could affect your business, you can develop a number of networks and monitoring efforts. You can join your industry's trade or professional organizations to learn what leaders in your industry are doing. You can become a member of your local chamber of commerce to monitor business trends and developments close to home. Other sources of information include trade shows, books in the popular press and government agencies.

- develop your product or service into a known brand

- determine which stage of the product life cycle you are in and to use this knowledge to better position your product or service

- assure that you develop effective product/service support through decisions regarding warranties, packaging, labeling, etc.

Part Two of this Challenge examines the marketing decisions involving place—decisions designed to make your products and services available to customers at the right times and places. The combination of these decisions often creates a competitive advantage because they cannot be easily duplicated by other businesses. Upon completion of Part Two you will be able to:

> *"A hamburger by any other name costs twice as much."*
>
> —Evan Esar

- determine how broadly your product or service must be distributed to reach the desired level of customer contact

- identify and select from a variety of distribution options based on the breadth of distribution you desire

- conduct a review of what location issues are important to providing customer satisfaction and to making appropriate location decisions

- examine additional convenience factors such as hours of operation, ease of ordering and ease of payment

Part Three of this Challenge explores the critically important issue of how to price your products and services to create a value that customers are willing to buy, while assuring your business acceptable profitability. Upon completion of Part Three you will be able to:

- relate the pricing decisions to the profile of your target market

- examine the effect of your pricing decisions on your company's image

- identify and review a variety of pricing strategies and learn to select the appropriate one(s) that will allow you to both provide customer satisfaction and maximum profitability

- examine related decisions such as discounts, allowances, deposits, rebates, etc. to determine their importance in your overall pricing strategy

PART ONE: Product Decisions

A product is anything offered to customers for acquisition, use, consumption or attention. It need not be a tangible item. Products can include services, personalities, places, organizations and ideas. Some products are combination goods, in that they have both a tangible and intangible component.

This publication will focus on marketing tangible and combination goods, services and places. However, many of the same concepts can be used to market personalities, organizations and ideas. The first step in tailoring the marketing mix is designing, developing and/or purchasing products which offer features and benefits that directly satisfy identified customer needs. Product decisions relate to assortment, warranties, branding, packaging and labeling.

Product Assortment

No matter what business you are in, the most crucial product decision you will face is what product(s) to manufacture or sell. That means more than choosing the right blend of products. To be competitive, a business must offer the quality its customers expect.

The key to choosing the right product assortment goes to the core of the marketing concept: satisfying the needs of customers. Before you can do that, you have to know what those needs are. You need to encourage constant feedback from your customers and employees, monitor returned goods, analyze complaints and lost sales, and identify "hot sellers" to find out what makes those products so popular.

To maintain a competitive advantage, your business needs to go one step further. You must deliver a product that exceeds the customers' expectations. That's what today's customers mean by value. Consider the success of the Little Caesar's pizza chain: it promises "Two great pizzas at one low price. Always! Always!"

Paradise Potions, Jim Copeland: We were hampered in the beginning by offering what we were told was "too narrow of a product line." Gee, we were struggling just to produce our first three products—a salsa, a ginger sauce and a flavored catsup. And yet the food wholesalers insisted that we had to become more important to the retailers. We

FYI

Examples of Products

Tangible goods: bakery goods, tires, lubricants, computers, boats, cheese

Services: haircuts, lawn care, house cleaning, car wash, dance lessons, dry cleaning, legal services, insurance

Personalities: actors, political candidates, athletes

Places: Downtown Eau Claire, a mall, university, hospital, resort, bank

Organizations: United Way, Red Cross, a political party

Ideas: "Just Say No" to drugs, "Buckle Up for Safety," "Don't Drink and Drive"

Combination: Orthodontic services, dinner in a restaurant, an oil change

have relied heavily on the same food tasting technique we started with—street-side samples from a cart—to receive consumer feedback on new product ideas. We have also run a couple of contests through our retailers, with a round-trip ticket to Jamaica for the best new "island" recipe.

Le Caribe Wholesalers, Marie Nelson: Our suppliers regularly bring new product ideas to us. Our role is more to critically review them and help the manufacturer decide how to position them in the food store than to create new products from scratch, although we did have success with a tropical jam we devised and brought to one of our manufacturers. Unlike most food brokers, we do regularly talk with food consumers in the aisles of food stores, at "taste of" events, and through some catering clients we work with.

Trade Winds Grocery, Jerry Lee: Staying up with consumer tastes is absolutely critical to our survival. We can't match the variety or prices of supermarkets, so we must compete on very responsive service. We do frequent in-store demonstrations with discount coupons being distributed. We solicit new recipes and product ideas through our cooking classes. We receive letters to the editor for our monthly newsletter. And we have a well-used and well-examined in-store suggestion box.

Profit Plus Accounting Services, Nancy Robinson: Accountants are not generally known for their "product assortment." Most provide the same basic package—monthly financial statements, checking reconciliations, tax return preparation and payroll accounting. We, of course, do all of these, but we go much further into the client's business by acting as a part-time chief financial officer. We meet monthly or quarterly to discuss upcoming financial decisions. We plan tax-saving strategies, we help install accounting software and we assist in making capital expenditure decisions.

Personal Workshop Preparation #18:
Our Product Assortment

Exceeding your customers' expectations does not come easily. It takes continual vigilance and a profound sense of never being totally satisfied with the benefits you offer through your products and services. It requires the ability to listen and then react appropriately.

The next Personal Workshop guides you through an examination of how you combine your product and services to provide the closest thing to total satisfaction for your customers.

In preparation for this Personal Workshop, examine how case study entrepreneur Jim Copeland completed this workshop.

Personal Workshop #18
Our Product Assortment

1. For your two highest dollar sales products or services, indicate the key customer need you are attempting to satisfy and detail the features and benefits you have built to achieve this satisfaction.

Product #1:

Paradise Potions—"Lightning Jack Caribbean Salsa"

Customer Need #1:

(Need of retailer) How to display, demonstrate and explain use of the product with complimentary food items.

Product Features:

(1) Recipe book available by calling 800 number, printed on all packaging, product literature, in-store displays and promotional coupons; (2) Effective coordination between product demonstrations-joint cooking presentations of several related products.

Product Benefits:

Once customers use product the first time, they can explore its culinary varieties through their own cooking guide. This makes for more informed customers when they shop the retail store. By cooperating with other product manufacturers, this product helps to build the awareness of the whole category of products.

Product #2:

Customer Need #2:

Product Features:

Product Benefits:

2. In what ways do you provide variety or breadth of choice for your product?

We offer multiple degrees of spiciness in a given sauce, as well as a variety of ingredient combinations. We also offer gift sets of two to three complimentary products.

3. Describe one change in features and/or benefits you have implemented in the past year that was the direct result of a customer complaint or suggestion:

> Adding the toll-free recipe line to our packaging.

4. Describe one modification in product features and/or benefits you have implemented in the past year as the direct result of actions by your competition:

> We now offer gift packs.

4a. How well received was this change?

> Exceptionally well for holiday time. Our post-sale consumer research indicates that our assortments of products greatly assists the novice gourmet cook in building a spice collection.

4b. If not well received, why not?

5. Describe how you believe your product features and benefits successfully exceed your customers' expectations:

> We offer a free condiment jar with every 32 oz. purchase of Lightning Jack salsa—a specialty serving piece most households do not own.

THE PURPOSE OF THIS WORKSHOP IS TO EVALUATE HOW WELL YOUR PRODUCT/SERVICE COMBINATION SATISFIES NEEDS EXPRESSED BY YOUR CUSTOMERS.

Personal Workshop #18
Our Product Assortment

1. For your two highest dollar sales products or services, indicate the key customer need you are attempting to satisfy and detail the features and benefits you have built to achieve this satisfaction.

Product #1:

Customer Need #1:

Product Features:

Product Benefits:

Product #2

Customer Need #2:

Product Features:

Product Benefits:

2. In what ways do you provide variety or breadth of choice for your product?

3. Describe one change in features and/or benefits you have implemented in the past year that was the direct result of a customer complaint or suggestion:

4. Describe one modification in product features and/or benefits you have implemented in the past year as the direct result of actions by your competition:

4a. How well received was this change?

4b. If not well received, why not ?

5. Describe how you believe your product features and benefits successfully exceed your customers' expectations:

Workshop Follow-Up

1. Reexamine how systematically you talk with customers, record their suggestions and act upon them. In the end, most customers not only want value but they also want to be appreciated.

2. Explore how useful your current system is for collecting competitive product information. Why reinvent the wheel if you can find a starting point from a competitor's actions?

3. Honestly evaluate how well you make your customers feel that they are receiving a surprisingly good value and unexpectedly good service.

New Products

New products are the lifeblood of your business. Customer demand and changing technology will affect how quickly products move through their life cycle. To keep a product assortment alive and current, you must continually freshen it with new offerings.

A new product may be a technical innovation for which you hold the patent. It may be a product that has been on the market for some time, but is new to your business. It may be an existing product that has undergone a "facelift" to keep it current.

Customers, employees, suppliers, trade and professional organizations, and even competitors are good sources of new product ideas. You can generate new ideas by:

- Surveying customers, employees, or suppliers

- Conducting contests for customers or others to generate new product ideas

- Reading professional publications and attending trade shows

- Observing what your competitors carry

Warranties

A **warranty** is a guarantee that a business will replace a product or refund all or part of the purchase price if the buyer finds it to be defective or lacking in some way. Warranties usually expire after a set period of time or use. Written warranties must conform with the rules of the Magnuson-Moss Warranty Act of 1975, so you may want to have your warranties reviewed by an attorney.

Key Word

Because they demonstrate that a business stands behind its products, warranties can serve as a competitive advantage. When a product's quality cannot be assessed until it is in use, guarantees reduce customer apprehension.

In addition to generating customer goodwill, warranties can provide valuable information about product reliability. You can keep track of returned or replaced products and correct or discontinue faulty ones. In a competitive marketplace, warranties can help a business right a wrong and keep a customer who might otherwise look elsewhere.

Branding Strategies

Key Words

A **brand** is a name, term, sign, symbol, design or some combination used to help customers recognize products/services and differentiate them from competing ones. Any component of the brand that legally cannot be used by another company is called a **trademark**. A product/service that is not branded is called a **generic product.**

Traditionally, manufacturers branded products only if they could ensure quality. Because most customers considered brand names to be of higher quality than unbranded products, they were willing to pay more for them. Manufacturers and middlemen marked up the prices, even though the differences between branded and unbranded products were often negligible.

Brand names don't offer that kind of magic anymore. Businesses no longer can charge top dollar for a product just because its name is well known. Today's consumers are savvy shoppers, and they balk at paying more for a brand name when lesser known or generic products are available. They tend to pay more only if they know a product offers exceptional value. Given this trend, you have three alternatives in branding decisions. You can choose an individual, family or licensed branding strategy. You may decide to use one strategy for one product and a different one for another.

When it is important to separate a product's identity from others offered by a business, an individual branding strategy is used. Examples abound in supermarket aisles. Proctor and Gamble, for instance, uses separate names for its laundry detergents to reflect the unique cleaning characteristics of the products. Mars sells a variety of candy products, all under different brand names.

Under the family branding strategy, a business uses the same name (usually the company's name or the name of one of its other products) on the products it produces or sells. This strategy is an effective way to save money and/or capitalize on the name and reputation of a popular existing product. Leinenkugel beer and Merkt cold pack cheese products are family branded. Many retailers, including Dayton's and K-Mart, have private label brands sold under a family brand name.

Businesses using a licensing brand strategy "rent" the name of an existing property from another business, instead of using a unique name. This strategy capitalizes on a well-recognized name. Anyone with children is familiar with the multitude of products licensed under the Teenage Mutant Ninja Turtles name. A business that wants to develop a line of Bucky Badger sportswear would have to "rent" the name and symbol from the University of Wisconsin-Madison.

Packaging

Packaging serves a variety of purposes. Products may be packaged to protect them from damage, to make inventory transport and storage easier, or to enhance their image. Packaging can make a product more functional or make it easier for customers to identify one's products in a sea of competitors. It can serve as a silent salesperson by identifying a product, offering information about it and/or folding into a point-of-purchase display.

If you offer services you also must consider packaging. Attractive uniforms for employees offer a clean and more professional image for a business and help customers identify employees. Other ways to package a service include designing signs, logos, stationery, store or office exteriors and interiors and displays on company vehicles.

> *"Every trend plants three seeds of the next one."*
>
> —Tom Hopkins

Labeling

Whether labeling is required by law or offered for customer convenience, it should be truthful and easy to read and understand. Labels should reflect the needs of customers. Graphics, colors, logos, and/or type styles should be chosen and executed to project the business' image.

Product Life Cycle

A product progresses through four stages: introduction, growth, maturity and decline. Technology, competition, and customer awareness and demand all play a role in how quickly a product moves through its life cycle. The life cycle of a product is illustrated in Figure 3.1.

Introduction: The product is an innovation and may have no direct competitors because of patents, technology or original concept. Sales are slow because most

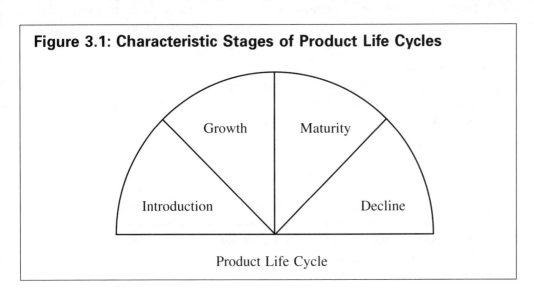

Figure 3.1: Characteristic Stages of Product Life Cycles

Growth   Maturity

Introduction   Decline

Product Life Cycle

customers don't know the product exists. Profits may be low because of the high costs of developing and promoting a new product.

Growth: Still relatively new, the product is beginning to experience direct competition. Its sales climb as customers become more aware of its existence. As sales climb, so do profits. Because competitive pressures are few, the product may produce its highest profits at this stage.

Maturity: The product has many direct competitors. Customers are familiar with it. To keep it fresh and current, new and improved versions may be introduced. Sales are beginning to peak. Direct competition is at its fiercest. Profits may begin to level off or decline.

Decline: The product approaches obsolescence as technology, changing needs and lifestyles advance. Demand is small. Only an occasional customer seeks it out. The product or service soon will be pulled off the market.

How long a product remains in each stage varies widely. Fads, like "Pet Rocks," move quickly from introduction to decline; the life cycle of a fad may be only weeks or months. Other products take several years to reach the maturity stage. Most products fall into this category, and they tend to remain at the maturity stage for many years.

FYI

Examples of Products in Various Stages of the Product Life Cycle

Introductory Stage

High resolution televisions, electric/battery-powered cars, genetically engineered fruits and vegetables, hypertext, artificial dietary fats used in food production, in-home computer shopping, medical products like Rogaine (for hair loss), distance educational learning programs

Growth Stage

Hydroponic vegetables, cellular phone services, environmentally aware products and packaging, compact discs, television shopping services, recycling services

Maturity Stage

Video rental service, health clubs, daycare services, hair salons, dental services, automobiles, computers, audio cassettes, most grocery products, legal services

Decline Stage

Black and white televisions, manual typewriters, wringer washing machines

From these examples, you should be able to determine where your product stands in its life cycle. Keeping track of product life cycles helps business owners keep product assortments up-to-date and points out the need to develop new products to replace those on the decline. It also aids in making pricing, place and promotional decisions for products.

How the Product Life Cycle Influences Your Marketing Decisions

If the product is in the introduction stage:

Product decisions

- Focus on branding strategies, choice of packaging, descriptive colors, logos and trademarks.

Pricing

- Consider price skimming or penetration pricing (See Part Two of this Challenge).

Place

- Devise strategies to get wholesalers and retailers to carry the new product.

If the product is in the growth stage:

Product decisions

- Emphasize ease of ordering, variety available, and accompanying service.

Pricing

- Prices begin to drop as product faces direct competition.

Place

- The number of distributors may increase as the result of rising consumer demand for the product and efforts to attract sales outlets. Distributors should be screened to ensure they're the right ones to carry the product.

If the product is in the maturity stage:

Product decisions

- Variations on the existing product create new excitement, make it more competitive, appeal to new target markets and/or bring it up-to-date.
- Package design can give the product a new look or make it more functional and/or appealing to a new market segment.
- Updating logos or symbols can give the product a new look or update its image.

Pricing

- Sales, discounts and other promotional pricing techniques become more important as prices continue to fall.

Place

- Consider strategies to get distributors to switch vendors; special trade, quantity and/or seasonal discounts; advertising allowances; contests or sweepstakes; cooperative advertising offers; and/or new product variations.

If the product is in the decline stage:

Product decisions

• Market the product as long as sufficient demand exists. It's only a matter of time before you pull the product from the market.

Price

• Promotional pricing can help to move the product.

Place

• There's no need to seek out distributors.

Personal Workshop Preparation #19: Where Are We in the Product Life Cycle?

Sometimes you do not want to face the fact that your product or service faces decreasing demand. By examining the characteristics of your current marketplace, you can discover opportunities to sell profitably even when your product's demand is in decline.

This Personal Workshop guides you through an examination of what stage of sales growth you face for your product or service.

In preparation for the next Personal Workshop #19, examine how case study entrepreneur Jerry Lee completed this workshop.

THE PURPOSE OF THIS WORKSHOP IS TO EVALUATE THE CURRENT STAGE OF GROWTH OF MARKET DEMAND FOR YOUR PRODUCT OR SERVICE.

Personal Workshop #19

Where Are We in the Product Life Cycle?

Select one choice for each question below:

1. Our product features are:
   ( ) Innovative and new
   (X) Copied by several competitors
   ( ) Offered by broad competition
   ( ) Not often found in the marketplace

2. Customer awareness of our product or service brand is:
   ( ) Still small, but growing
   (X) Well established in "pockets" of the market
   ( ) Widely known across the U.S
   ( ) Has been declining

3. Our annual dollar sales growth for our main product line has been:
( ) Growing in excess of 20% per year recently
(X) Growing by 10-20% per year recently
( ) Growing by less than 10% per year recently
( ) Declining recently

4. In the past year, our profitability has been:
( ) Greatly reduced by development costs
(X) The best ever
( ) Starting to level off
( ) Declining

5. We introduce new product designs and features:
(X) At least twice per year
( ) At least once every other year
( ) Once in the past three years
( ) Not in recent memory

THE PURPOSE OF THIS WORKSHOP IS TO EVALUATE THE CURRENT STAGE OF GROWTH OF MARKET DEMAND FOR YOUR PRODUCT OR SERVICE.

Personal Workshop #19
Where Are We in the Product Life Cycle?

Select one choice for each question below:

1. Our product features are:
( ) Innovative and new
( ) Copied by several competitors
( ) Offered by broad competition
( ) Not often found in the marketplace

2. Customer awareness of our product or service brand is:
( ) Still small, but growing
( ) Well established in "pockets" of the market
( ) Widely known across the U.S
( ) Has been declining

3. Our annual dollar sales growth for our main product line has been:
( ) Growing in excess of 20% per year recently
( ) Growing by 10-20% per year recently
( ) Growing by less than 10% per year recently
( ) Declining recently

4. In the past year, our profitability has been:
   ( )   Greatly reduced by development costs
   ( )   The best ever
   ( )   Starting to level off
   ( )   Declining

5. We introduce new product designs and features:
   ( )   At least twice per year
   ( )   At least once every other year
   ( )   Once in the past three years
   ( )   Not in recent memory

Workshop Follow-Up

1. If you generally checked the first box for each question:

It is likely that you are a relatively new company or have introduced a very innovative new product line. This can be a frustrating time period, because you are starting to experience the great potential market demand for your product but your profits are lagging, often because of the substantial investments you have had to make in equipment, space, personnel and promotional programs. Hold on and be patient, the profit will come!

2. If you generally checked the second box for each question:

Your product or service is in the growth stage of market demand. This is the stage where you reap your greatest profit, as demand for your product often outruns your ability to supply it. Reliable suppliers, a very dependable order department and outstanding customer service are critical in this stage.

3. If you generally checked the third box for each question:

Your product or service has most likely entered the maturity stage of its growth. It is time to create a new, improved version with fresh marketing. You are starting to be taken for granted somewhat by your customers. Allying yourself with the best distributors is critical to continued profitability because you face frequent and ferocious new competition.

4. If you generally checked the fourth box for each question:

Your product or service is probably facing obsolescence and is considered old and out-of-date by the broad part of the market. If you are a low cost producer with a well-established distribution system you may be able to extract some profit for several more years. The best advice: take your past profits and invest in a new, innovative business.

Learn how to introduce new products from the entrepreneuerial owner of a successful new product development company, in *From Concept to Market*, Gary S. Lynn, New York: John Wiley & Sons, Inc., 1989.

PART TWO: Place Decisions

Place decisions are designed to make products and services available to consumers at the right times and places. They offer an important competitive advantage because they cannot be easily duplicated by other businesses and often can result in a strong feeling of superior interest in the need for convenience by the customer.

> *"Good is not good, where better is expected."*
>
> —Thomas Fuller

Degree of Market Exposure

You must decide whether your product will be sold in every appropriate location (intensive distribution) or only at selected ones (selective or exclusive distribution). How customers buy a product determines its degree of market exposure. Examine what type of products benefit from each of the following styles of distribution.

Intensive Distribution

Intensive distribution is the right choice when convenience is more important to customers than price, prestige, or product information. Products that are distributed intensively are purchased frequently, so customers are familiar with the brand and usually don't seek additional information from distributors about them.

The following approach tends to characterize intensive distribution:

- Marketers believe that customers view their products as commodities and will switch quickly to a comparable brand if theirs is out-of-stock.

- They must take measures to ensure that their products are easy to find and always available.

- Since the product is sold in many different locations, the promotional burden falls on the manufacturer to make special allowances to retailers that promote their brand.

Selective Distribution

These are products for which a customer will shop around. Customers tend to buy these products infrequently, so it is harder for them to distinguish between brands. Typical information that a buyer may seek before making a purchase are price, features, service comparisons, types of use, fit, and/or accessories.

Products that Usually Require Intensive Distribution

Consumer products	Industrial products
canned goods, soft drinks, cigarettes, newspapers, film development, gasoline	office supplies, paper products, cleaning supplies, copying and FAX services

Marketers of selectively distributed products tend to exhibit the following behavior:

- They are very selective about where they place their products.

- They evaluate distributors by their financial stability, longevity in the market, quality of sales force and ability to maintain the products' image.

- They assure that customers receive the information they seek by developing special sales training programs and material for distributors.

- They share the burden of promoting the product with the retailer. The manufacturer does that by keeping its brand name before the public and helping the retailer generate sales. The retailer must let consumers know the product is available and help them gather the information they need to make a buying decision.

Exclusive Distribution

Exclusive distribution is a channel strategy in which one vendor has exclusive rights to distribute a product in a specific geographic area. These arrangements are often formalized in contracts between manufacturer and retailer. Products that benefit from exclusive distribution tend to be expensive, complex and/or in need of special service. Businesses considering exclusive distribution should use the same criteria for evaluating retailers as they would in selective distribution arrangements.

Channels of Distribution

A channel of distribution is a series of firms or individuals that help move products and services from the producer to the user. Customer needs determine whether a product is sold through direct or indirect channels. The role business owners play in those channels affects their marketing plans and the prices they can charge.

Types of Wholesalers and Retailers

Wholesalers buy products from the manufacturer for resale to other wholesalers, retailers or businesses. In addition to selling goods, they may store,

Products that Usually Require Selective Distribution

Consumer products	*Industrial products*
clothing, shoes, furniture, computers, home entertainment equipment, tax services, auto repair services, appliances, jewelry	copy machines, FAX machines, computers, office furniture, accounting services, cleaning services and supplies

regroup, transport, gather and communicate information, and participate in financing.

Wholesalers also may develop unique product lines to sell to others in the channel. There are two types of wholesalers:

Merchant Wholesalers: own the goods they sell. They also perform a variety of other marketing functions. Examples: drop-shippers, rack jobbers, producers' cooperatives, specialty wholesalers and mail-order wholesalers.

Agents: do not take title to the goods they distribute, but they do perform other marketing functions. Examples: brokers, auction companies, manufacturers' agents.

Retailers buy goods from manufacturers and/or wholesalers and sell them to consumers. They attempt to bring together an assortment of goods that will appeal to their target customers. Like wholesalers, they may perform a number of marketing functions. Examples: department stores, mail-order companies, computer shopping services, vending services.

Direct Channel of Distribution

With direct channel of distribution, goods pass directly from the producer to the end user. Either the producer or the end point performs all marketing activities; there are no middlemen, no wholesalers or retailers in the channel. Direct channels of distribution give the producer the greatest control over how a product is marketed. Because the producer sells directly to the consumer, he or she gets quick, precise customer feedback.

Products sold through direct channels are generally highly perishable, expensive and/or complex. Most services are sold through direct channels because they tend to be inseparable from the service provider. That means service providers must carefully select and train their employees to ensure that the service they provide is at the quality level customers demand.

Products that May Benefit from Exclusive Distribution

Consumer products

cars, tax services, recreational products, computers, appliances, expensive perfumes and cosmetics, designer clothes

Industrial products

copy and FAX machines, computers, office furniture, accounting and brokerage services, agricultural and road construction equipment

Indirect Channel of Distribution

With indirect channel of distribution, goods move from producer to consumer via wholesalers and retailers. These "middlemen" are selected based on their ability to reach customers and perform a variety of marketing functions.

Producers of goods that require intensive distribution use indirect channels as an efficient means of reaching all possible users. Producers may choose to distribute their products using indirect channels if they are unable or unwilling to perform certain marketing functions. In effect, these producers "hire" wholesalers and retailers to carry out these duties for them. Because contact with consumers is limited, producers who sell through indirect channels must take steps to ensure they do not lose touch with the needs of their final customers.

Channel Considerations

The selection of the most efficient channel for your business will be determined by a number of different factors. The primary consideration, however, is your type of business.

For Manufacturers

Market exposure

• Will I use an intensive, selective or exclusive distribution for my products?

Channel of distribution

• Which wholesalers and/or retailers should I choose to distribute my products?
• What marketing functions should they perform?
• What marketing functions do they expect from me?

Business location

• Where should I locate my business?

Days and hours of operation

• What days and hours should I be open?

FYI

Marketing Functions Performed by Members of the Channel of Distribution

• Buying
• Selling
• Transporting
• Financing
• Communicating
• Information gathering
• Re-grouping (accumulating, bulk-breaking, sorting, assorting)

For Distributors

Market exposure

- Who else carries this product?

Channel of distribution

- Who will I buy my products from?
- What marketing functions do I want other channel members to provide?
- What marketing functions do I provide?

Business location

- Where should I locate my business?

Days and hours of operation

- What days and hours should I be open?

For Service Providers

Market exposure

- Who else provides this service?

Channel of distribution

- Should I affiliate with a franchise?
- What marketing functions do I want other channel members to provide?
- What marketing functions do I provide?

Business location

- Where should I locate my business?

Days and hours of operation

- What days and hours should I be open?

Paradise Potions, Jim Copeland: One of our most pressing requirements when we started was to attract the attention and interest of an aggressive food wholesaler. The average food wholesaler is presented with 100 or so new products per month. If you are not known in some way, your chances of getting a shot are slim. We knew we had to attract substantial attention. We did this through a diversified publicity campaign, which included an appearance on the Home Show on network television. This led to local publicity from which we heard from Jerry Lee, owner of the Trade Winds Grocery. While doing taste tests at Jerry's store, we were discovered by Marie Nelson of Le Caribe Wholesalers who just so happens was looking to expand their representation of genuine "island" cuisine. Even though we do not have an official contract that says so, we are using Le Caribe as our exclusive distributor to retailers in a five-state area. We are now exploring growth into the corporate gift and incentive market and most likely we will have to find a second distributor, as Le Caribe really doesn't do this type of selling.

 Le Caribe Wholesalers, Marie Nelson: We, of course, try to gain exclusive distribution for all of our products, but rarely achieve this because we are still fairly small and regional in our selling. Many food wholesalers perform only the basic marketing functions for their manufacturers—shelf stocking and inventory checking, new product presentation to buyers, credit checking and collection follow-up and some point-of-sale promotion. We take a more active role, in that we strongly suggest new product innovations backed by specific promotional programs. We educate the buyers to the unique capabilities of our manufacturers. And we aggressively push in-store taste testings, demonstrations and cooking classes.

 Trade Winds Grocery, Jerry Lee: Our lifeblood is the effective combination of sharp buying on food staples and the latest, most stylish food concepts in the Spanish and Caribbean submarkets. We walk a fine line between not being important enough to our large suppliers, such as Progresso soups, and seeming too big to be interested in new, innovative food product developers. We can't stock every new product, of course, so we rely heavily on wholesalers like Le Caribe to "filter out" the best new food producers. We then give every viable new product a chance to show what it can do in our store. We are looking not only for initial sales, but also for very excited consumer feedback.

 Profit Plus Accounting Services, Nancy Robinson: Many of my accounting colleagues are relatively passive in their marketing. They often pick up clients by doing their corporate tax work then work into other areas such as payroll accounting, financial consulting and accounting automation. Although many accountants use specially designed software to handle their tax work, few align themselves with a particular software company to become a certified dealer. One of the ways we differentiate ourselves is by becoming a certified support center for Peachtree PC-based accounting software. This certification required stringent study and testing, as well as semi-annual trips to Atlanta to receive upgrades. We were also required to bring on a full-time marketing support individual who was approved by Peachtree. It is relatively unusual for an accountancy to receive this certification, so we are proud of ours.

Location

Location can be very important to a small business. For businesses in consumer markets, the right location may be the only way to attract buyers as promotional opportunities are severely limited. With the advent of just-in-time inventory systems, manufacturers may find that a location near customers is a competitive advantage that can save time and money.

Where a business locates depends on customer needs, space requirements, local ordinances and zoning laws, and site availability.

Following are some of the local resources you may find helpful in collecting location information are:

- The local chamber of commerce often runs an exchange listing of available industrial and office space.

- Drive around neighborhoods where you think you might like to be located. Note the names and phone numbers of the management companies and call to ask about available space.

- Explore industrial parks by dropping into medium-sized manufacturing buildings to see if they have space they would sublease to you.

- Check out the zoning regulations for your area by contacting your city or town planning or zoning departments. They can tell the zoning status of every parcel of land in your municipality.

Use the following checkpoints to determine if you have addressed all location concerns in your marketing strategy:

1. Businesses in Industrial Markets

( ) **Customer access:** Are you located near your customers?

( ) **Labor supply:** Does the area offer laborers skilled in your line of work? Are job training facilities and programs available?

( ) **Price of labor:** What are the going wages in the community? Can you hire quality workers at a fair wage?

( ) **Access to resources:** Is there an adequate and inexpensive supply of water, electricity and other basic resources? Are the utilities and resources you need on or near the site?

( ) **Access to transportation and storage facilities:** Can you move goods quickly and inexpensively? Are inexpensive storage facilities nearby?

( ) **Availability of land:** Is the site large enough to meet your current and future needs?

( ) **Governmental support:** Do local governmental leaders support business and its needs? Are taxes reasonable? Are zoning laws and local ordinances conducive to your business?

( ) **Winning track record:** What other businesses are located nearby? Are they successful? If not, why not? Does their experience point out problems with this site?

2. Businesses in Consumer Markets

( ) **Customer access:** Are you located near your customers?

( ) **Location near complimentary businesses:** Is the site near businesses that serve the same types of customers as yours? (For example, a shoe store might want to move next door to a women's clothing store.)

( ) **Parking:** Is parking convenient and adequate for your customers?

( ) **Entrance and exit:** Can customers easily enter and leave your business? Does traffic pose a problem at any time during the business day?

( ) **Labor supply:** Does the local market offer the quality workers your business requires?

( ) **Price of labor:** What are the going wages in the community? Can you hire quality workers at a fair wage?

( ) **Access to resources:** Is there an adequate and inexpensive supply of water, electricity and other basic resources? Are the utilities and resources you need on or near the site?

( ) **Winning track record:** What other businesses are located nearby? Are they successful? If not, why not? Does their experience point out problems with this site?

( ) **Governmental support:** Do local governmental leaders support business and its needs? Are taxes reasonable? Are zoning laws and local ordinances conducive to your business?

FYI

Ways to "Extend" Business Hours

1. Install mail drops so customers can return products when you are not there.

2. Use an answering service, answering and/or FAX machine to record messages when no one is in.

3. Open later in the day and stay open later in the evening.

4. Produce catalogs so customers can call or mail in orders.

5. Put an employee "on call" on weekends.

6. Hire part-time employees to work at night. Give them other jobs to complete at times when business is slow.

Days and Hours of Operation

A common complaint among small town merchants is the lack of business during the day. Considering that those are the hours when most people are working, it's no surprise that sales are down. Many businesses are open when they want to be open—not when their customers want them to be open.

Who determines your business' days and hours of operation—you or your customers? The evolution of consumers' lifestyles and an increasingly competitive environment dictate that small businesses must be open when their customers need and want to buy their products.

Personal Workshop Preparation #20: How We Get Our Product to the Customer

It is increasingly clear that both consumers and business customers often possess more money than time. And the available time must be split between obtaining needed information on a product or service, finding a supplier, contacting the supplier, ordering the product, paying for the product and receiving the product.

The relative ease of completing all of these steps in one place, at one time is a major reason for the astronomical growth of mail order and catalog sales in America. In recent years, there has been substantial growth in business sales by catalog. Today there are several suppliers who sell paper through catalogs—who would have imagined selling such a commodity product this way?

Because convenience has become the first or second most important purchase criteria, wise choice of distribution channel and location strategy are critical to your success as a small business.

To examine how well your current distribution strategy satisfies your customers' needs, complete the next Personal Workshop. To prepare, examine how case study entrepreneur Jerry Lee from Trade Winds Grocery completed this exercise.

Personal Notes

_____

_____

_____

_____

Trade Winds Grocery

THE PURPOSE OF THIS WORKSHOP IS TO EXPLAIN WHAT TYPE OF DISTRIBUTION STRATEGY YOU PURSUE.

Personal Workshop #20
How We Get Our Product to the Customer

1. Our products require:
   ( ) Extensive distribution
   (X) Selective distribution
   ( ) Exclusive distribution

   1a. Explain your feelings for the above distribution strategy:

   Our lifeblood is the effective combination of sharp buying on food staples and the latest, most stylish food concepts in the Spanish and Caribbean submarkets. We walk a fine line between not being important enough to our large suppliers, such as Progresso soups, and seeming too big to be interested in new, innovative food product developers. We can't stock every new product, of course, so we rely heavily on wholesalers like Le Caribe to "filter out" the best new food producers. We then give every viable new product a chance to show what it can do in our store. We are looking not only for initial sales, but also for very excited consumer feedback.

2. We:
   (X) Sell directly to customers
   ( ) Use distributors and/or wholesalers to sell
   ( ) Use manufacturers sales representatives to sell

3. Physical location is important to our marketing strategy:
   Yes (X)   No ( )

   3a. If Yes, describe how you use physical location to draw attention to your business:

   We are located near the restored downtown business district of a college town with more than 50,000 in population. We are immediately next to the largest dry cleaner in town, which encourages our shoppers to visit our store when they are dropping off or picking up their cleaning.

4. We have good availability of affordable, trained labor in and around our chosen location.
   Yes (X)   No ( )

   4a. If No, describe how you overcome this drawback to your location:

5. Close proximity to our suppliers is very important to our marketing strategy:
   Yes (X)   No ( )

   5a. If Yes, describe how you have arranged your location to facilitate transactions with your suppliers:

   We must have dependable daily delivery of more than 1,000 different products, and yet we try hard to keep our inventory costs down so as to be able to offer competitive prices on the most widely shopped items.

Personal Workshop #20
How We Get Our Product to the Customer

1. Our products require:
   ( ) Extensive distribution
   ( ) Selective distribution
   ( ) Exclusive distribution

   1a. Explain your feelings for the above distribution strategy:

2. We:
   ( ) Sell directly to customers
   ( ) Use distributors and/or wholesalers to sell
   ( ) Use manufacturers sales representatives to sell

3. Physical location is important to our marketing strategy:
   Yes ( )   No ( )

   3a. If Yes, describe how you use physical location to draw attention to your business:

4. We have good availability of affordable, trained labor in and around our chosen location.
   Yes ( )   No ( )

   4a. If NO, describe how you overcome this drawback to your location:

5. Close proximity to our suppliers is very important to our marketing strategy:
   Yes ( )   No ( )

   5a. If Yes, describe how you have arranged your location to facilitate transactions with your suppliers:

Workshop Follow-Up

 1. Reexamine what convenience means to your target customers. For example, are they willing to drive some distance to visit a retailer who carries fewer varieties of what they want, but offers better inventory and useful recipes and demonstrations of how to use the products, many of which are unfamiliar to most customers?

 2. Explore additional distribution routes you could pursue to broaden the market for the products you offer, for example, opening a catering operation, providing local corporation dining rooms, etc.

PART THREE: Pricing Decisions

Price is the dollar value customers are willing and able to pay for goods and services. It may be paid as fees, dues, rent, tuition, interest, or the selling price of tangible goods and services.

What Pricing Should Do

> *"When I started this business, I just put the price I wanted to charge on each item. I always wondered why some products sold better than others. Funny how many things can affect your prices when you are really informed."*
>
> —The Late Learner, Small Business Management Fundamentals, Dan Steinhoff

Many business owners think that setting price is a one-dimensional process—simply add up your costs, throw in a little for profit and publish the total as your pricing. Pricing can affect your business in many ways, some not so obvious at first. Effective pricing strategy results in pricing that:

- is the result of the combination of image, service, product features and profit
- is justifiable in terms of customer expectations
- includes terms of sale, discounts, and allowances
- uses breakeven analysis
- often connotes quality
- is only part of your competitive edge

All pricing decisions hinge on the answer to the question: What is it worth to the customer? The factors that customers use to evaluate the price of goods and services are described in Table 3.1.

Staying competitive demands that you continually measure the value of your product or service. Ask yourself: Is it faster, cleaner, more compact, etc.?

 FYI

How can you turn your business location into a competitive advantage? For innovative ideas and an answer to this question, read *Marketing Without Advertising* by Michael Phillips and Salli Rasberry, Nolo Press, 1989.

Table 3.1: Prime Price Considerations for Customers

Here are some factors customers consider as they decide whether the price is right for your products:

1. Prior experience with your products and those of the competition.

2. Word-of-mouth information about your reputation and products from family, friends and others.

3. Information from comparison shopping of brands and outlets.

4. "Clues" they associate with your business and products:

   • Your business' appearance inside and out, cleanliness of rest rooms, convenience for shopping;

   • Appearance and professional qualifications of your staff and their quality of service; and

   • Quality of advertising and other external communications.

5. Value of services and/or products added, or "bundled," to main product.

6. Situational influences:

   • Purchase for a special occasion, when price is not an overwhelming factor;

   • An emergency purchase, when there is no time to shop;

   • A product of convenience, in which customers will pay more if it saves time; and

   • Impulse purchases.

The Key to Successful Pricing

FYI

To set prices, business owners must know all the costs of producing and/or selling products and how much target markets are willing and able to pay for them.

Identifying and allocating all expenses associated with products is an accounting problem, requiring financial investigation. An experienced small business accountant can help you develop a system to perform this sleuth work on a monthly or quarterly basis.

Business owners who understand their target markets can better figure out how much customers are willing and able to pay for products. Table 3.1 above illustrates some factors that influence how customers determine what that "right price" is.

The Fallacy of Price Cutting

Some small businesses, when not guided by a pricing strategy, will attempt to outdo competition by cutting their prices. These businesses believe that this will increase the number of units they will sell and thereby increase their total revenue. This is most often a fallacy, primarily because price is rarely the most important criteria a customer uses to decide whom to buy from. As a result, lowering your price below your competition often has no effect on the buying behavior of your customer and only results in reduced profit for your company.

> *"Everything is worth what its purchaser will pay for it."*
>
> —Publilius Syrus

Among the common reasons that companies use to justify price reductions are:

- "It is easier to sell if it is less expensive." This is often a mark of laziness.
- Habit. You have always cut prices when pushed.
- You are afraid of losing a customer.
- A new competitor has come into town.
- It seems to affect your profitability relatively little. This often appears to be the case because you don't really know how much it costs you to make the product or service.

What then is the alternative to cutting price when under customer or competitive pressure?

> *"Anybody can cut prices, but it takes brains to produce a better article."*
>
> —Philip Daniel Armour

To answer in a short phrase: "Put more features in!" Don't take price out. Put more satisfaction into the product or service. You can do this by improving product design, decreasing quality defects, providing better after-sale service, offering a wider selection of products, and making it more convenient to buy from you.

Pricing products and services is not an exact science. However, all pricing decisions are based on a common concept: Prices must be at least high enough to cover costs and overhead and make a profit.

Strategy and Your Business' Image

The price a business charges for its products must be consistent with the image it hopes to project. While price alone is usually not the primary motivation for buying, customers often make a direct connection between your product's pricing category and their sense of quality, for example:

High-quality product @ low price = low-quality image

This perception is especially true for medical, legal and other professional services in which customers often cannot assess the level of quality provided. Table 3.2 outlines marketing strategies for high- and low-priced products.

Table 3.2: How Prices Affect Business Image

If you charge a high price for a product, you must:

1. Ensure that advertising and other cues reinforce an image of high quality.

2. Explain why your prices are higher by educating customers and emphasizing your experience, track record and/or state-of-the-art equipment.

3. Continually monitor the quality of the products/services you provide. If your customers are paying top dollar, you had better exceed their expectations.

If you charge a low price for a product, you must:

1. Ensure that other elements of the marketing mix (product quality, branding, packaging, place decisions, advertising, etc.) back up the bargain image.

2. Offer real value (most customers don't want low quality, even if they pay low prices).

3. Explain in advertising how your business can offer such low prices.

4. Monitor the quality of products/services you provide. As a minimum, you must meet your customers' expectations for quality to keep their confidence—and repeat business.

Be Aware: A word of caution for business owners trying to provide the lowest priced product in the market: That competitive advantage can be easily matched by the competition. Larger competitors with "deep pockets" can take advantage of quantity discounts by buying in bulk. And customers who base shopping decisions on price alone are generally not loyal customers. They are always shopping around for a better price.

Preliminary Thoughts on Setting Price

Successful pricing balances your need to cover all pertinent costs with the willingness of the market to buy. When you are new in business, there may be very little relationship between what it costs you to produce your product or service and what customers will pay for it. Remember, you are proving yourself to these people at this point.

Market research, if done well, can tell what price level the market would likely accept. Further research informs you of typical costs of production and selling you will face in your marketplace. If you feel that you cannot make a high enough return on your investment, you will know it before you invest your money.

If your business has been around for awhile, it can be useful to reexamine the totality of costs you incur to bring the product to market against the trend in your pricing to see if your profitability has been heading up or down. Some businesses continue to try to operate, despite shrinking profitability, because they cannot focus on how to add additional worth to their product.

Be Aware: Don't fall into the trap of pricing solely by "formulas," such as the retailer who simply doubles the wholesale cost or the services supplier who prices based on achieving a target dollar amount per hour.

Procedure for Setting Prices

The following steps will assure that you systematically consider all market requirements when you set your pricing. Personal Workshops for each step follow this outline.

STEP 1: Set Price Floor

- Determine all costs for marketing, production and distribution
- Use breakeven analysis

STEP 2: Set Price Ceiling

- Determine the market's price sensitivity
- Look at competitors' prices
- Talk to customers and potential customers

STEP 3: Set Pricing Objectives

- Recover upfront costs quickly
- Gain market share
- Consider image
- Examine economies of scale

STEP 4: Select Pricing Strategy

- Price skimming
- Penetration pricing
- One price vs. flexible pricing
- Time of purchase

- Odd vs. even pricing
- Price lining
- Product bundling
- Tie-ins and metering

STEP 5: Select Discount Policy

STEP 6: Select a Geographic Pricing Policy

- FOB Factory
- Freight absorptions
- Uniform delivered price
- Zone pricing

Personal Workshop Preparation #21: How We Set Our Prices, Steps 1 - 6

The following Personal Workshop guides you through the six important steps to take as you examine all aspects of your company's pricing.

Use the manufacturing and service companies as examples when you complete the "how to" exercises. Then try your newly acquired pricing information on your own business.

Six Step Personal Workshop #21
STEP 1: How We Set Our Prices

Introduction

This Personal Workshop requires some explanation and mathematical examples to aid you in crafting a comprehensive pricing strategy.

Instead of completing Personal Workshop #21 in one set of questions, you will examine techniques for establishing each of the six key components of pricing strategy, review some examples of mathematical calculation and then you will illustrate and describe how you have completed each of the six steps for your company's pricing strategy.

Examine each of these steps as you review how you have built the pricing schedule for your products or services.

Set Price Floor—The "How To"

Many managers use cost-based pricing as a starting point, deviating from it as necessary to reflect market reality. Your first step is to examine your costs:

Fixed Costs

Expenses that do not usually depend directly upon the sales level. **Fixed costs** include rent, lease payments, heating, telephone, advertising, etc.

Variable Costs

Expenses that tend to vary according to the sales volume are considered **variable costs**. To determine, ask yourself: If I don't sell anything in the next month, what costs must I still pay?

Example 1:
Reliable Chair—Identify Fixed and Variable Costs

Monthly Fixed Costs:		Variable Costs:	
Building rent	$ 18,000	Direct materials	$ 28,800
Property tax	4,000	Direct labor	26,400
Utilities	900	Overtime labor	1,500
Telephone	850	General maintenance*	1,300
Insurance	500	Billing costs	2,000
Advertising	3,000		
Office salaries	7,000		
General maintenance*	700		
Total	$ 34,950	Total	$ 60,000

* 35% fixed/65% variable

Exercise 1: You Try It!
West Window Shade—Identify Fixed and Variable Costs

Note: For each expense below designate whether it is a Fixed or Variable expense by circling the letter V or F.

Expense Category	$ Amount	Circle — Variable or Fixed	
Office salaries	$ 5,000	V	F
Direct labor	30,000	V	F
Office supplies	500	V	F
Telephone	100	V	F
Insurance	400	V	F
Sales commissions	10,000	V	F
Rent	2,000	V	F
Advertising	250	V	F
Maintenance	1,250	V	F

Key Words

Answers:
See
Workshop
Follow-Up
on p. 155.

Breakeven Analysis

Breakeven is the hypothetical point where sales income and expense just equal each other. The following steps will show how to calculate your breakeven point:

Key Word

1. Determine total monthly fixed costs.

2. Take the price of the product for which you wish to calculate breakeven. Determine the variable costs/unit assignable to this product.

3. Subtract the variable costs-per-unit from the product's selling price. This dollar amount represents the proportion of a typical sale available to pay fixed expenses, also known as the "contribution."

4. Divide the total monthly fixed costs by the "contribution" per unit sold.

5. This number represents the number of units of this product you must sell per month to cover all of your fixed and variable costs.

Example 2:
Reliable Chair—Calculate Breakeven in Units

Data:

- Our total fixed costs = $ 34,950

- Our total variable costs = $60,000

- Our selling price per unit = $250

- Our total estimated annual sales = 600 units

1. Calculate variable cost per unit =
   Total variable costs ÷ number of units sold
   $60,000 ÷ 600 = $100 per unit.

2. Contribution per unit =
   Selling price - variable cost per unit
   $250 - $100 = $150 per unit

3. Calculate breakeven points in units =
   Total fixed costs ÷ contribution per unit
   $34,950 ÷ $150 = 233 units

Exercise 2: You Try It!
West Window Shade—Calculate Breakeven in Units

Data:

- Our total fixed cost = $7,400

- Our total variable costs = $42,100

- Our selling price per unit = $25.00

- Our total estimated annual sales = 4,000 units

1. Calculate variable cost per unit =
   Total variable cost ÷ number of units sold

2. Contribution per unit =
   Selling price - variable cost per unit

3. Calculate breakeven point in units =
   Total fixed cost ÷ contribution per unit

Answers:
See
Workshop
Follow-Up
on pp.
155-156.

Breakeven analysis can also be used to determine what effect a change in price will have on the units that must be sold to still achieve breakeven.

Example 3:
Reliable Chair—Using Breakeven to Set Prices

1. Reliable's sales staff is asking for a price reduction of $25 due to competitive price pressure.

2. Before deciding to lower the price, the sales manager wants to determine how many more chairs they will have to sell in order to maintain the breakeven point.

3. To do this calculation, he starts with the total fixed costs his operation faces: $34,950.

4. He then determines the contribution per unit by taking the proposed new price, $225 and subtracting the variable costs per unit (see Example 2) of $100 to arrive at a figure of $125 per unit.

5. He then divides the total fixed costs, $34,950 by the contribution per unit of $125 to arrive at a breakeven unit volume of 279.6 or 280 units.

6. At $250 per chair, the company had to sell 233 units to breakeven. After a $25 per unit price reduction, they must sell 280 units to achieve breakeven. Whether they can do this depends upon how well they execute their marketing strategy.

Exercise 3: You Try It!
West Window Shade—Using Breakeven to Set Price

1. Assume the selling price is lowered from $25 to $23.

2. How many more window shades must they sell to breakeven if the price is reduced $2 per unit?

3. New breakeven in units: _____

   (Use this space for calculation)

Using Breakeven to Determine Profitability

Although learning how to calculate breakeven is helpful to projecting the effects of various pricing scenarios, the real reason you are in business is to make as much profit as you legally can. The same breakeven analysis techniques you have already used can be applied to determining how many units or dollars of sales your company must make in order to achieve a certain profit. Examine the example below to see how this done:

Example 4:
Reliable Chair—Using Breakeven to
Determine Profitability

1. Assume Reliable's sales management wishes to make $50,000 profit from selling its chairs. Assume also that the selling price is $250/unit.

2. Start by adding the desired profit to the total fixed costs—$34,950 + $50,000 = $84,950.

3. Use the contribution per unit of $150 that you previously calculated to divide into the total of the profit and fixed costs—$84,950.
   $84,950 ÷ $150 = 567

4. You would have to sell around 567 chairs to cover all of your costs and make a $50,000 profit. This may require quite a bit of sales effort!

Exercise 4: You Try It!
West Window Shade—Using Breakeven to
Determine Profitability

1. Assume West Window wants to make a $5,000 profit on shades that sell for $25 each. What is its unit breakeven point?

2. Unit breakeven: _____

   (Use this space for calculation)

Answers:
See
Workshop
Follow-Up
on p. 156.

Be Aware: Just because you can calculate the unit breakeven point for a particular profit goal does not mean that your plant can physically produce that number of units in the time allowed. So, apply some realistic production thinking before you start to count your profits.

THE PURPOSE OF THIS WORKSHOP IS: TO ALLOW YOU TO DETERMINE YOUR PRICE FLOOR BY USING KNOWLEDGE OF YOUR FIXED AND VARIABLE COSTS AND BREAKEVEN ANALYSIS.

Six Step Personal Workshop # 21
STEP 1: How We Set Our Prices

Setting the Price Floor

1. Our total annual fixed costs are: $_____

2. Our total annual variable costs are: $_____

3. Our desired total dollar profit for the next year is: $_____

4. Our estimated annual unit volume of sales is:

   Product #1: $ _____

   Product #2: $ _____

   Product #3: $_____

Note: If your company sells a line of products or services, you may wish to calculate breakeven separately for each of the main product categories, therefore you will want to repeat this analysis several times.

5. Our variable cost per unit is:

   Product #1: $ _____

   Product #2: $ _____

   Product #3: $ _____

6. Our projected selling price per unit is:

   Product #1: $ _____

   Product #2: $ _____

   Product #3: $_____

7. Our profit contribution per unit is:

Product #1: $ _____

Product #2: $ _____

Product #3: $ _____

8. Our breakeven in units is:

Product #1: $_____

Product #2: $ _____

Product #3: $ _____

Note: If you wish to calculate separate breakeven points for several products, you will need to establish some method by which to assign a certain amount of your total fixed costs to each product. This is often done by determining the direct labor that goes into each product and using this percentage of total labor cost to break down the fixed expenses.

This Personal Workshop continues with Step 2

Six Step Personal Workshop #21
STEP 2: How We Set Our Prices

Set Price Ceiling—The "How To"

Factors Affecting Price Sensitivity

• Unique Value Effect

Buyers are less sensitive to a product's price the more they value any unique attributes that differentiate it from competing products. For example:

- Cartier Jewelers: High society clientele; one of a kind designs
- SONY appliances: Very reliable; incorporate latest designs

It can require extensive advertising to communicate your unique differences. For example, Perdue Chicken runs major TV ad campaigns to drive home that, "It takes a tough man to make a tender chicken."

• Substitute Awareness

The more substitutes for your product that a customer perceives, the more they are sensitive to your price. Ask yourself:

- What alternatives do buyers have?
- Are buyers aware of the alternative suppliers?

• The Difficult Comparison Effect

Buyers are less sensitive to price when comparison with competing offers is difficult. Ask yourself:

- Can the attributes of our product and those of competitors be observed? Or must the customer buy the product first?
- Is our product highly complex, requiring specialists to compare it with others?
- Are our prices and those of competition easily comparable? Or are there a variety of sizes and/or combinations to be considered?

• The Total Expenditure Effect

Buyers tend to be more price sensitive when the purchase is larger, say over $100. Ask yourself:

- How significant are our buyers' expenditures both in dollar terms and as a percentage of their incomes?

• The End-Benefit Effect

Buyers are more sensitive to the price of the product when the product's price accounts for a larger share of the total cost. For example: A manufacturer of office desks who buys sheet metal for fabrication will be more sensitive to changes in the sheet metal cost as its customers become more sensitive to the price of its desks.

• The Price-Quality Effect

Buyers are less sensitive to price to the extent that a higher price signals that the product is of higher quality. A low price can be so associated in the customer's mind with low quality, that the low price can prevent sales.

Look at Competition

Before you attempt to make pricing comparisons with your competitors, do whatever you can to learn enough about their products and marketing to determine if what they offer is sufficiently similar to what you offer. Unequal offers should not be priced the same usually. Use the following guides to determine how to react to competitors' pricing:

• Price above competition when:

- Your market is not price sensitive.
- Your market consists mainly of growing businesses.
- Your product is an integral part of an established system.
- You have a strong reputation for status, service or high perceived value.
- Your product cost represents a small percentage of your customer's total costs.

- Price below competition when:

    - Your market is sensitive to price changes.
    - You are attempting to enter a new market.
    - Your customers need to reorder.
    - Your business is small enough so that lowering prices won't start a price war.
    - You have not yet reached full production capacity.

THE PURPOSE OF THIS WORKSHOP IS TO DETERMINE THE MAXIMUM PRICING YOU FEEL IS APPROPRIATE FOR YOUR MARKETING OBJECTIVES, LEVEL OF COMPETITION AND FINANCIAL OBJECTIVES.

Six Step Personal Workshop #21
STEP 2: How We Set Our Prices

Setting the Price Ceiling

1. Do your customers consider your product or service:
    ( ) Fairly common
    ( ) Very unique

2. How aware are your customers of substitutes for your product:
    ( ) Not very aware
    ( ) Very aware

3. How easy is it for your customers to compare your product with competition:
    ( ) Not very easy
    ( ) Very easy

4. How significant is the dollar amount spent by your customers on your product or service as a proportion of their total expenditures in a year:
    ( ) Not very significant
    ( ) Very significant

5. How aware are your customers of the time and or money that can be saved by buying your product:
    ( ) Not very aware
    ( ) Very aware

6. How closely tied in your customers' minds is your price and their sense of quality:
    ( ) Not very closely tied
    ( ) Very closely tied

7. When examining your competitors, which of the following are true:

7a.

( ) You are one of a number of growing companies

( ) You are new in the marketplace

7b.

( ) You need to be known in the marketplace

( ) You are happy to be overlooked by competition

Note: If you largely checked the first boxes, you may be able to price slightly above your competition; if you checked the second boxes, you will most likely have to price below your competition until you become more well established.

This Personal Workshop continues with STEP 3

Six Step Personal Workshop #21
STEP 3: How We Set Our Prices

Set Pricing Objectives—The "How To"

A common objective is to attempt through your pricing to recover your development investments as quickly as possible. This is particularly critical in industries where competition can make your product obsolete in a short period of time.

Some companies set pricing with an eye toward encouraging widespread trial of the product when it is first introduced. The assumption is that when the price is increased, customers will remain loyal because the product fulfills their needs.

The role pricing plays in your company's image is important to consider. An inappropriate price can undo other marketing aimed at a certain image.

Often as your sales increase, your costs decrease at some definable point. Your pricing objective may be to sell enough units quickly so as to reach that point of reduced cost as soon as possible.

THE PURPOSE OF THIS WORKSHOP IS TO DESCRIBE WHAT FINANCIAL GOALS YOU WHICH TO ACHIEVE AND HOW YOUR PRICING WILL BE DESIGNED TO AID IN SUCCESS.

Six Step Personal Workshop #21
STEP 3: How We Set Our Prices

Setting Pricing Objectives

1. Have you recently made a large expenditure to develop or acquire a new product?
( ) Yes   ( ) No

1a. If yes, what dollar amount of investment would you like to recover?
$ _____

1b. Over what time period do you hope to do this?

1c. What unit sales volume do you expect over this period?

1d. What selling price per unit must you charge to recover your investment?
$_____

2. Is one of your main marketing goals to gain market share quickly?
( ) Yes   ( ) No

2a. If yes, what price level do you believe you must set, relative to competition, to attract significant interest among prospective customers?
$_____

3. Is your pricing an important part of your image marketing?
( ) Yes   ( ) No

3a. If yes, describe how you use pricing to substantiate your level of product quality:

4. Do your per unit costs drop significantly at some level of production?
( ) Yes   ( ) No

4a. If yes, what is that unit or dollar purchase volume level?

4b. How must you set your price to reach this level in the near future?

This Personal Workshop continues with STEP 4

Six Step Personal Workshop #21
STEP 4: How We Set Our Prices

Pricing Strategies—The "How To"

It is attractive to use a formula to set your pricing. However, be careful to consider four key factors before you finalize your prices:

- Your direct and indirect operating costs
- Your competition's product/service features and its prices
- Your desired marketing image
- Your need to gain a certain return on investment

Commonly used formulas, such as doubling your wholesale cost, often fail to take into consideration all of these factors.

The following pricing approaches are appropriate for a wide variety of business. Examine each and determine which scenario most closely supports your company's marketing objectives.

Price Skimming

This is a price-setting scheme that permits maximum profit to be gained because the product's perceived value is much more important to the customer than its economic value.

For example: The Apple Newton handheld computer commanded premium pricing when first introduced because of its uniqueness and promise to better organize the users life.

Penetration Pricing

This approach uses a deliberately low price to introduce the product, to induce trial by customers, with the expectation that loyalty to the product will develop sufficiently to permit the gradual raising of prices.

Be Aware: Your competitors can neutralize your price advantage by dropping their prices below yours. They may be less likely to do this, however, if your company enjoys a discernible cost advantage, or if your company is small enough so as to not attract attention of larger competitors.

For example: Little Caesar's Pizza bombarded the marketplace with "two pizzas for the price of one" when entering the market, with the intent of pulling away Domino's customers, who are not renowned for being pizza gourmets, but who love deals.

Neutral Pricing

This marketing scheme attempts to set prices pretty much like everyone else, so that price becomes secondary in the customer's purchase decision. This is a highly preferred strategy for many small businesses, particularly new ones who are offering largely undifferentiated products.

For example: The local carpet cleaning company who offers "three rooms for $39.95" is usually priced very close to competitors. The company wants to sell on the basis of quick response, ability to remove stains, etc., rather than price.

One Price vs. Flexible Pricing

This is a pricing option that requires fairly skilled salespeople who can discern from direct contact what combination of standard product features, delivery and customization each customers wishes. To facilitate such pricing, "packages" are often created in advance of the sale to make it more easily understood by the customer.

For example: Travel agents commonly offer several prices for the same cruise: "budget," "standard" and "deluxe." The main differentiating factor is usually the size and location of the stateroom, plus the inclusion of some high-perceived value perks, such as dining with the captain.

Pricing by Time of Purchase

When your customer base is made up of segments that shop at different times, you may be able to adjust pricing by the hour of the day.

For example: "Early Bird" dinner discounts.

Price Lining

This strategy involves offering a line of related products with a progression of prices.

For example: Sears, Roebuck & Co. has made billions of dollars of sales by offering products priced as "Good," "Better" and "Best." For many years their "Best" was a Sears private-label product.

Product Bundling

This approach requires the customer to buy a product or service they may not deem the most important in order to get the product or service they deem most important. There are two approaches:

- Optional Bundling: Products can be bought separately, but the option is available to buy them together for a discount.

For example: Ski equipment can be bought piece by piece, but is often sold as a set for a price below the total of the prices for the individual pieces.

• Value-Added Bundling: Offers an additional value to price sensitive buyers.

For example: Alcoa sells aluminum in cable for less than it sells virgin aluminum.

Tie-Ins and Metering

• Tie-ins are now illegal in many cases, but some products are designed so that only their replacement parts will fit.

For example: Movie theaters commonly require patrons to purchase their snacks on the premises at premium prices.

• Metering is pricing based on renting an asset rather then selling it.

For example: Some photocopiers are leased for a fixed monthly payment plus a usage charge based on the copying volume.

THE PURPOSE OF THIS WORKSHOP IS TO SELECT ONE OR MORE PRICING STRATEGIES AND DESCRIBE THEIR IMPORTANCE IN YOUR OVERALL MARKETING STRATEGY.

Six Step Personal Workshop #21
STEP 4: How We Set Our Prices

Selecting a Pricing Policy

1. Is your desired product positioning to:
   ( ) Take advantage of the perceived superiority of your product
   ( ) Gain the maximum market share as quickly as possible

2. Based on your desired product positioning, designate which pricing policy is more suitable to your objectives:
   ( ) Price Skimming
   ( ) Penetration Pricing

3. Do you intend to have a single price or price list for your products, at all times?
   ( ) Yes   ( ) No

3a. If No, indicate how you will differentiate your pricing for different product/service combinations:

4. Is time of purchase an important factor in determining your pricing?
   (   ) Yes   (   ) No

5. If yes, how will you select your pricing to allow for different prices at different times?

6. Do you intend to establish "pricing families" for related products?
   (   ) Yes   (   )No

6a. If yes, describe how you will set this pricing:

7. Do you intend to offer different pricing for products individually and as a group?
   (   ) Yes   (   ) No

7a. If yes, describe how you will set pricing for product or service groupings:

8. Do you intend to use tie-ins or metering arrangements as part of your pricing?
   (   ) Yes   (   ) No

8a. If yes, describe how this pricing arrangement will be integrated into your marketing strategy:

This Personal Workshop continues with STEP 5

Six Step Personal Workshop #21
STEP 5: How We Set Our Prices

Select a Discount Policy—The "How To"

Customers today expect some reduction in price for buying in certain combinations, at certain times or by exceeding certain dollar or unit amounts. This is a fact of life and if you are to succeed in setting profitable pricing, you must take discounts into consideration.

Often discounts are utilized to expedite the payment for orders, such as the common "one percent, 10 days, net 30" which allows a 10 percent discount on the amount invoiced if it is paid within ten days of being received. But be cautious in offering discounts. Many larger customers have a bad habit of taking the discount even if they don't pay within the required ten days. The net effect of the discount in these instances is to just reduce your profit.

The basic strategy of a discount is to encourage your customers to buy more at one time or buy more often because they save money when they do so.

There are a number of well known discount strategies:

Noncumulative

This is a discount from the established price for buying in certain quantities.

For example: 13 donuts for the price of 12.

Cumulative

In this discount arrangement, the customer earns a reduction in pricing based on total purchases over a specified period of time, such as annually. These are often known as volume discounts.

For example: A car dealership that gives 10 percent off normal pricing once you buy more than $500 of maintenance and repairs.

Step

To receive this type of discount, the customer must buy a minimum dollar amount first, then receives the discount on each dollar purchased above the minimum. These are also known as block discounts.

For example: A printer offers copies at one half the normal cost per page after 100 copies of a single sheet have been made.

Trade

These are discounts granted for a wide variety of customers, based on set discount schedules. Sometimes the maximum discount is offered for non-returnable sales.

For example: Book publishers routinely offer 20 percent or greater discounts on relatively small quantities of books—fewer than 30 copies. The maximum discount for books is usually 50 percent if more than 50 copies are bought at one time and if they are bought on a non-return basis.

Promotional

This type of discount is used to motivate the customer to join in the promotion of your product through their advertising. A common discount is two percent of your invoice if they submit proof that they ran ads with your logo in them.

For example: Sony pays retailers large amounts of money to display its logo in all advertising, promotion and signage.

THE PURPOSE OF THIS WORKSHOP IS TO DESCRIBE UNDER WHAT CONDITIONS YOU WILL GRANT A DISCOUNT IN YOUR PRICING.

Six Step Personal Workshop #21
STEP 5: How We Set Our Prices

Choosing a Price Discount Plan

1. Which of the following will you use to set discounts:
   (   ) Total dollar sales of an individual order
   (   ) Total accumulated dollar sales over a period of time
   (   ) All dollar sales over a minimum amount
   (   ) For documented promotion using your product or service name

2. Do you offer a discount for paying quickly?
   (   ) Yes   (   ) No

2a. If yes, what is the percentage discount? _____ percent
And what is the payment time?: _____

3. Do you offer standard discounts to anyone who orders a specified dollar amount?
   (   ) Yes   (   ) No

3a. What is this discount?

4. Do you offer larger discounts once a new customer has ordered a certain number of times?
   (   ) Yes   (   ) No

4a. What are these discounts?

This Personal Workshop continues with STEP 6

Six Step Personal Workshop #21

STEP 6: How We Set Our Prices

Select a Geographic Pricing Policy—The "How To"

Sales often are lost, not because your basic price isn't acceptable, but because the cost of transporting your product to the customer was higher than that of your competitors.

For example, in the corrugated box business, once the shipping distance becomes more than 150 miles from the plant, the freight cost becomes uncompetitive. As a result, in the most industrial parts of the U.S. you will find box factories every 200 to 300 miles.

Freight costs can easily run two to four percent of the total cost of your product, so you need to have a system for tracking these costs and using the results to negotiate better transportation rates from common carriers and air freight companies. You should also take into consideration your customers' habits regarding how quickly they expect delivery after placing their order.

A number of business-oriented mail order catalogs have realized that very prompt delivery is critical to maintaining an image of a highly responsive marketer. As a result, you now commonly see mail order businesses offering an overnight delivery option, often for only $1 more than customary ground delivery.

Another factor to consider in geographic price strategy is that your competition may not be equally strong throughout the entire geographical area in which you sell. Certain cities may be ferociously competitive and others may have little competition. This variation may allow you to price slightly higher in some markets to compensate for pricing elsewhere that prevents you from recovering all of your transportation and handling costs.

There are a number of geographic pricing strategies:

FOB Factory

FOB stands for "free on board," which means the seller is free of responsibility once the goods are on board the delivery vehicle.

In this scheme, the buyer pays the freight from your production location to his or her warehouse. Legally, the customer assumes title to the goods when they are loaded onto the truck at your factory. This can be a vital fact if the load is damaged in-transit.

For example: A furniture manufacturer sends its truck into a component suppliers plant to pick up materials. Once the materials are loaded, they are owned by the customer who is responsible for paying the truck freight to get the load back to his or her plant.

Freight Absorption

In this pricing approach, you deduct the transportation costs from your customer's total invoice. This approach usually requires the customer to buy a minimum dollar quantity to receive the deduction.

For example: Some office supply warehouse chains offer free local delivery for any order over $50.

Uniform Delivered Price

This is the opposite of the FOB Factory approach in that you, as the supplier, pay the transportation but add it to your total price. You are legally responsible for the load until it reaches your customer's facility. Quite often zones are used to establish the transportation cost, which reduces the complexity of calculating the total price.

For example: This approach is commonly used with imported products, where the "landed" cost includes ocean and domestic truck freight to get the shipment to a customer's plant.

THE PURPOSE OF THIS WORKSHOP IS TO ALLOW YOU TO DESCRIBE HOW YOU WILL TAKE TRANSPORTATION COSTS INTO CONSIDERATION WHEN SETTING YOUR PRICING.

Six Step Personal Workshop #21
STEP 6: How We Set Our Prices

Selecting a Geographic Pricing Policy

1. What is the traditional method in your industry of including freight costs in overall pricing?
   ( ) FOB Factory
   ( ) Freight Absorption
   ( ) Uniform Delivered Price

2. Are you able to modify your pricing in different parts of your distribution area?
   ( ) Yes   ( ) No

2a. If yes, describe how you do this:

3. Do you use zones in determining what freight cost to add to your pricing?
   ( ) Yes   ( ) No

3a. If yes, describe how you do this:

4. What different types of transportation do your customers demand?

---

5. How do you track the costs of these various methods?

6. How do you use this costing information to negotiate better rates?

Workshop Follow-Up

This summary is designed to allow you to review all of the key points to consider when setting your company's pricing.

 1. Put into place a reliable system for capturing expense information so that you can accurately describe your fixed and variable costs.

 2. Combine your expense information with estimated unit sales for your product to complete one or more breakeven analyses. This technique can be used to determine how many units must be produced to cover costs, as well as how many units must be sold to permit a certain profit amount.

 3. Use the breakeven analysis to set the minimum price per unit of product or service you must sell. Avoid going below this point.

 4. Utilize market intelligence and your experience to evaluate the pricing and product feature combinations of your most direct competitors. Analyze how price-sensitive your desired customer segments are. Use this information to determine how far above the minimum you may go with your pricing.

 5. Describe the financial goals—sales and profits—you wish to achieve with your pricing. Particularly consider the product development costs you wish to recover. Detail over what time period you wish to repay these expenditures. Don't forget to also consider non-financial goals for your pricing, such as its impact on your overall marketing image.

 6. Review industry practices, customer demands, your financial and market growth goals and any special relationships your company may enjoy with key customers to select one or more of the pricing strategies described previously. You may weave a combination of several strategies together.

 7. Acknowledge discount policies in your industry as well as specialized demands for discounts from your larger customers. Determine how you can

 FYI

Share the experience and knowledge of a panel of successful small business owners when they discuss price setting strategies in the book *Small Business Survival Guide,* The Prentice Hall Editorial Staff, Prentice Hall, ISBN # 0-13-045329-3.

offset these price reductions through more efficient handling, better raw material purchasing, etc. in order to maintain your desired profit level.

 8. Explore whether you must charge one standard price across the whole geographical area you cover. Are there variations in competition that may permit higher prices in certain areas? Examine how well you know your transportation costs. Ask yourself: Are your customers paying their fair share of the freight? If not, how can you adjust this situation?

Answers to Personal Workshop #21 Step 1

Exercise 1: You Try It!
West Window Shade—Identify Fixed and Variable Costs

Note: For each expense below designate whether it is a Fixed or Variable expense by circling the letter F or V.

Expense Category	$ Amount	Circle Variable	Fixed
Office salaries	$5,000		F
Direct labor	30,000	V	
Office supplies	500	V	
Telephone	100		F
Insurance	400		F
Sales commission	10,000	V	
Rent	2,000		F
Advertising	250		F
Maintenance	1,250	V	

Exercise 2: You Try It!
West Window Shade—Calculate Breakeven in Units

Data:

- Our total fixed cost = $7,400

- Our total variable costs = $42,100

- Our selling price per unit = $25.00

- Our total estimated annual sales = 4,000 units

1. Calculate variable cost per unit =
   Total variable cost ÷ number of units sold
   $42,100 ÷ 4,000 = $10.53 per unit

2. Contribution per unit =
   Selling price - variable cost per unit
   $25.00 - $10.53 = $14.47

3. Calculate breakeven point in units =
   Total fixed cost ÷ contribution per unit
   $7,400 ÷ $14.47 = 512 units (rounded)

Breakeven analysis can also be used to determine what effect a change in price will have on the units that must be sold to still achieve breakeven.

Exercise 3: You Try It!

West Window Shade—Using Break-even to Set Price

1. Assume the selling price is lowered from $25 to $23.

2. How many more window shades must they sell to break even if the price is reduced $2.00 per unit?

   a. New contribution per unit = $23 - $10.53 = $12.47
   b. Total fixed costs = $7,400
   c. Divide $7,400 by $12.47 = 594 (rounded up)
   d. This is the new breakeven point in units

3. New breakeven in units: 594.

Exercise 4: You Try It!

West Window Shade—Using Breakeven to Determine Profitability

1. Assume West Window wants to make a $5,000 profit on shades that sell for $25 each. What is its unit breakeven point?

   a. Total of desired total fixed costs plus profit = $7,400 + $5,000 = $12,400

   b. Contribution per unit is $14.47 at a selling price of $25 per unit

   c. Divide total of profit and fixed costs—$12,400—by the unit contribution—$14.47

   d. You would have to sell 857 shades in order to reach the desired profit amount

2. Unit breakeven: 857

You Have Completed Challenge 3

In Challenge 1, you combined your existing knowledge of your customers' profile and their needs with new market research to ascertain the answers to marketing questions that will allow you to create an even more powerful marketing strategy.

In Challenge 2, you systematically elaborated on this strategy through the completion of comprehensive written marketing planning that detailed your company's financial and market share goals and the techniques you expect to use to achieve them.

In Challenge 3, you detailed very specific sets of tactics for creating the product design, selecting the distribution arrangement, and calculating the pricing required to achieve optimum profitability.

To use the vernacular, this is where "the rubber meets the road." This Challenge was designed to assist you in developing the detailed set of action steps that will energize you and your employees to drive forward, all committed to the same set of goals and steps to reach them.

You may have heard the expression, "the devil is in the details." Your ability to produce the desired profitability goals for your company is inexorably connected to your ability to successfully execute the many details of everyday marketing when not everything goes as planned, when you are under tremendous competitive pressure, and when you never have enough money.

The detailed action plan you have started in Challenge 3 will be completed with the work you will do in Challenge 4: Communicating With Your Market. In Challenge 4 you will detail the techniques you will use to communicate effectively to customers how your product, place, and pricing policies are superior to those of your competitors.

You Leave Challenge 3 with the Following:

Information: You have been exposed to many detailed procedures for guiding new product development, evaluating location decisions, capturing operational costs, and a multi-step process for combining realistic costing information, competitive profiles, and customer requirements to achieve profitable pricing.

Tools: The Personal Workshops you have completed are the tools you will use to make your marketing decisions pertaining to product, place, and pricing.

Learning: You have learned techniques for capturing and effectively using market information, particularly product features desired by your target customers, their demands for convenience in buying, and the costs you incur to satisfy their demands.

Networking: Throughout this Challenge you have been exposed to resources for collecting information useful in developing a coordinated marketing mix. Included are sources of information on developing new products, establishing warranties, relating product features to your position in the product life cycle, gaining necessary information on selecting a location for your business, and sources of facts and figures useful for establishing profitable pricing.

Challenge 3 Self-Assessment

The following self-assessment guides you through a checklist of activities you should be able to complete before you attempt to implement your marketing plan.

**Pages
105-119**

PART ONE: Product Decisions

( ) I can explain the rationale behind our product assortment.

( ) I can describe how we conduct new product development.

( ) I can present any brand-oriented marketing we perform and describe how we compare with competition.

( ) I can describe our packaging and labeling strategies.

( ) I can explain our warranty/guarantee policies.

PART TWO: Place Decisions

**Pages
119-130**

( ) I can explain how broadly we feel we must distribute our products.

( ) I can describe how we select the type of distribution we use for our products and how this strategy relates to our goals for market share growth.

( ) I can present our rationale for choosing the locations for our facilities, how we expedite customer orders and payments, and how we obtain sufficient personnel, and all the steps we take to assure that our customers receive our products quickly and in good order.

( ) I can explain our policy on hours of operation and relate it to customer needs.

PART THREE: Pricing Decisions

**Pages
130-156**

( ) I can detail our fixed and variable expenses and identify our breakeven points for all of our product lines.

( ) I can explain the goals we wish to achieve with our pricing strategy.

( ) I can present how our pricing strategy flows from our market research, and how our pricing is used to reinforce our desired marketing image.

( ) I can describe the specific pricing strategies we use and why.

( ) I can explain variations in our pricing due to discounts, consideration of transportation costs, and geographic differences in customer demand and competitive pressure.

Take Another Look

Record anything from your Challenges, your Personal Workshops, or your personal reflections that you want to remember.

Review the results of your Challenge 3 Self-Assessment. Which areas do you still need to work on? Follow up on these areas by reviewing appropriate sections of this Challenge.

Challenge 4

Communicating With Your Market

"I wouldn't hesitate for a second to choose the plain-looking ad that is alive and vital and meaningful, over the ad that is beautiful but dumb."

—Bill Bernbach, creator of the original Volkswagen ads and
"We try harder because we are No. 2" campaign for Avis

You have built a "better mousetrap," but customers are not beating a path to your door. Advertising media representatives are calling you suggesting that if you just advertise in their newspaper or magazine, or on their radio or television station, customers will flock to your business. How do you decide where you should advertise, or whether you should advertise at all?

Most promotion and advertising decisions are made on a whim. Often the sales ability of the media representative is the most important factor in determining whether to advertise. Promotions are not coordinated, and follow up is nonexistent.

Upon completion of Challenge 4 you will be able to:

• Develop the foundation for your promotion plan

• Understand the difference between features and benefits

• Position your product/service/store

• Develop a message that will be effective

• Determine what promotional tools will work for your specific business

• Use those promotional tools

• Obtain synergy from your promotions

The Foundation for Your Promotion Plan

Before you can use promotion effectively, you must have the answers to the following questions: otherwise, all the creativity in the world will not make your promotions effective.

159

- Who are your most likely customers?
- What are their needs and wants?
- What are they willing to pay for?

The major mistake that many businesses make is not sufficiently differentiating their customer bases and developing product and promotional strategies for each one. Another mistake businesses make is selecting a group of customers that are almost impossible to reach. Try finding an advertising media or mailing list that includes all people who are thinking about starting a business, and excludes those who are not considering entrepreneurship. You may need to define your target market in some other manner in order to determine how to reach them. To target people interested in starting a new business, you may target an occupation where you feel a high percentage of people will have an interest. For example, many school teachers and bureaucrats are interested in starting a small business.

Looking at Your Business: Strengths, Weaknesses, Image

First look at the strengths and weaknesses of your business from your customer's point of view. Remember that we do not live by reality, but by our perception of reality. If your customers perceive you have a weakness, you can't just ignore it if they are wrong.

On a regular basis, those inside the business should take a close look at sales staff, customer contacts, phone service, hours of operation, products and services, building and parking, and billing. Then, they should ask their customers about those same issues.

Once business owner/managers have compared their perspective to that of their customers, the next step is determine how to improve that image.

Developing Your Promotional Plan

- Who are your competitors?
- What are their strengths and weaknesses?
- Why do customers buy from them?

As important as focusing on the customer is, a firm must also base its strategies on its strengths in view of its competitors' strengths and weaknesses. It makes

FYI

Continually, small business owners ask, "Should I advertise in this publication or on this station?" when the question should be, "What is the best use of my promotional dollar?" The problem is that this means you have to explore all advertising media and all promotional tools available to determine the answer.

little sense to go square up against a more formidable opponent. If a small firm is facing off against a stronger competitor, it should avoid imitating the competition's strategy and tactics.

You answered these questions about your competition as you were developing your marketing plan. Now take a look at how you are going to use the information. It is quite possible that you will decide you have to further define your most likely customers, increase your understanding of their needs, or collect more information on your competition before you can develop the message you want to communicate to your customers. The more completely you answer these questions, the easier it will be to develop your message and select your promotional tools.

Answering these questions is just the first step in developing your promotional plan. As with your marketing plan, you need to determine what you want to do. Of course you want to generate sales. But not all promotional tools can generate sales for all industries. Some create awareness, some generate inquiries, some qualify leads, some nurture potential customers, and some sell. So there are four additional questions to answer before you develop any promotional campaign. These questions are just common sense. The problem is they are so common sense that we often overlook them.

Four Critical Questions in Planning a Promotional Campaign

1. What do you want to happen?

- Sell Your Product or Service

- Generate Leads

- Qualify Leads

- Reinforce Selling

- Create Awareness

2. Why do you want it to happen?

- Develop a mailing list

If you define your market as anyone who lives in Dane County, every newspaper, magazine, radio station, television station, and coupon pack can tell you that they reach your market exactly. And they will all be correct. So your media selection will be comparing apples to oranges.

If you define your market as males, 25 to 54, with an interest in participating in athletic activities, you will automatically rule out some of the media. And by obtaining media kits, you will be able to determine which media reaches this market most cost effectively.

- Generate leads for telemarketers
- Qualify leads for sales force
- Reopen doors to lost customers

3. How will you know if it happens?

- Tracking responses
- Asking customers

4. What will you do if it happens?

- Follow up with telemarketing
- Follow up with sales call
- Send additional information
- Put leads on newsletter list
- Put leads on mailing list

Promotional Goals

Promotional goals can be either short-term or long-term. Short-term promotional goals are targets that a business owner hopes to realize in a year or less; long-term goals take longer to achieve.

> *"Many a small thing has been made large by the right kind of advertising."*
>
> —Mark Twain

Short-term promotional goals are a call to action. They should aim to generate immediate responses from customers. Each promotion should have a specific response in mind. Not all promotions will generate sales. Promotions can be designed to do the following:

Sell Your Product or Service: This promotion must tell the whole story; it is the salesperson, and a response device is critical. See how Jim Copeland used direct mail to sell his products.

 Paradise Potions, Jim Copeland: We sent a direct mail piece to all the wholesalers that carry our products offering a special deal on a new flavored dip. The direct mail piece included testimonials from food experts who had tried the new dip, as well as pricing information. Of the 50 wholesalers that carry our products, 10 placed an order for the new dip.

Generate Leads: This promotion gives less detail; the piece arouses interest in the product or service but it lets the sales force tell the story; typically a gift, free item, or coupon is offered to increase response; often used to legally "steal" names from a purchased list. See how Marie Nelson used an ad to generate leads for her business.

Le Caribe Wholesalers, Marie Nelson: We wanted to expand the number of grocery stores that we serviced. We placed an ad in *Progressive Grocer* offering a free report on "Ethnic Food Trends in the United States."

Qualify Leads: This promotion gives less detail; the piece arouses interest in the product or service but it lets the sales force tell the story; the response device provides information to qualify the leads received; will get a lower response rate but more qualified leads than a promotion which generates leads. Marie Nelson used a second ad to qualify leads.

Le Caribe Wholesalers, Marie Nelson: Upon following up on the leads generated by our ad in *Progressive Grocer*, we found that many of the stores who responded had their inventory purchased at a regional headquarters. So our next ad offered a special discount on products if the stores responded by our deadline. Once the store mailed or called in their response, a sales person contacted the store to close the sale.

Reinforce Selling: This promotion repeats and reinforces the sales message; the eye remembers better than the ear; gives detailed/technical information, between-call contact, provides background information; offers news of changes or late-breaking developments. Follow the technique Nancy Robinson used to reinforce selling.

Profit Plus Accounting Services, Nancy Robinson: I send a quarterly newsletter to both my clients and prospects. Besides educating the readers, the purpose of the newsletter is to distinguish myself from all the other accountants I compete with.

Create Awareness: This promotion is used for general marketing such as sending reprints, stay in-touch newspapers; it tries to build a pen pal relationship. See how Jerry Lee was able to create awareness about his business.

Trade Winds Grocery, Jerry Lee: We ran an advertisement in the local newspaper to inform people that Trade Winds Grocery was the place to find unusual food items.

Long-term goals might call for establishing a product's image or educating customers about a product or the business' image.

Personal Workshop Preparation #22: Promotional Goals

Use the next workshop to help you categorize your short-term promotional efforts by the goal they help to achieve. Many businesses find that their promotions generate awareness, but don't help to achieve lead qualification or sales. You will see what holes you have to fill, and begin to evaluate how you can more effectively use your promotional dollar.

Over the last two years, the promotional expenditures of Paradise Potions increased significantly. Owner Jim Copeland decided to analyze his promotions to see if he could make better use of his promotional dollar. Before you begin the next workshop, take a look at how Jim Copeland completed it.

THE PURPOSE OF THIS WORKSHOP IS TO DETERMINE FOR EVERY PROMOTION YOU CONDUCTED LAST YEAR, WHICH PROMOTIONAL GOAL IT HELPED TO ACHIEVE. BE HONEST—ADVERTISING CAN NOT DIRECTLY SELL A PROFESSIONAL SERVICE.

Personal Workshop #22
Promotional Goals

Promotion	Generate Leads	Qualify Leads	Reinforce Selling	Create Awareness	Directly Sell
New flavored dip mailing					X
Ad in *Progressive Grocer*			X		
Sales calls on prospective wholesalers		X			
Booth at national food products trade show	X	X		X	X

Consider eliminating or modifying any promotions that only created awareness. Check off the promotions you need to reconsider. By consciously thinking about the purpose of your promotions, you will be better able to objectively decide which promotions work for you and which do not. This will allow you to modify promotions to make them work harder or eliminate them altogether.

THE PURPOSE OF THIS WORKSHOP IS TO DETERMINE FOR EVERY PROMOTION YOU CONDUCTED LAST YEAR, WHICH PROMOTIONAL GOAL IT HELPED TO ACHIEVE. BE HONEST—ADVERTISING CAN NOT DIRECTLY SELL A PROFESSIONAL SERVICE.

Personal Workshop #22
Promotional Goals

Promotion	Generate Leads	Qualify Leads	Reinforce Selling	Create Awareness	Directly Sell

Consider eliminating or modifying any promotions that only created awareness. Check off the promotions you need to reconsider. By consciously thinking about the purpose of your promotions, you will be better able to objectively decide which promotions work for you and which do not. This will allow you to modify promotions to make them work harder or eliminate them altogether.

Workshop Follow-Up

You can now begin to consciously think about the purpose of every promotion. Thinking in this way will encourage you to make your promotions work harder for you. Rather than placing an ad that just generates awareness, you will design the ad to also generate inquiries, qualify leads, or sell.

What is Communicated—The Promotional Message

Key Words

There is an important difference between features and benefits of a product or service. A **feature** is a physical characteristic of your product or service. It tells what your product does, how your product works, or what services you provide. Features are the language of your company. For example, the features of a desk include: made of wood, 4 drawers plus a file drawer, and 3 feet wide by 6 feet long.

Benefits translate features into the customer's language. A benefit tells customers what they will gain from the features of your product. The benefit is the reason why the person will buy your product or service. For example, the benefits of the desk translate into a status symbol or enhanced professional image, easy access to materials and files, and enough room to work.

Marketers often try to increase the perceived benefits of a product by stressing quality. But quality in itself is not a benefit or selling point. You need to find out what comprises quality and prove it—don't just say it. Ford's Quality is Job #1 is an exception to this rule because Ford started with this slogan before quality was an overused term.

Those using a mass marketing approach often throw benefits at potential customers, hoping that one will generate interest in their product or service. Those using a multiple target market approach will select different benefits to appeal to the different groups they target.

FYI

Hamburgers, fries, soft drinks, etc. are the features that McDonald's sells. McDonald's uses a multiple target market approach. But people go to McDonald's for different reasons, so the benefits it promotes to each group are different.

Kids Under 8
Kids don't go to McDonald's for the food; just take a look at how much food is eaten. As a matter of fact, often kids do not consider going through the drive through at McDonald's. Kids go to McDonald's for the fun. So that is exactly what McDonald's sells them during Saturday morning cartoons.

Kids 9 to 18
Although the members of this group may have enormous appetites, the reason they go to McDonald's is not for food. They go to McDonald's to socialize with their friends. So McDonald's emphasizes "Food, Folks and Fun" in its prime time advertisements.

Adults
McDonald's may not be the place adults would choose to eat. But when you are starving and running late, driving through McDonald's is very convenient. So McDonald's advertises "Breakfast on the Run" during morning drive time.

McDonald's understands that people do not buy the features of what it sells, but the benefits. And for each group, the benefits may be different.

Personal Workshop Preparation #23:
Features vs. Benefits

The goal of this workshop is to learn to talk the language of your customers. Being knowledgeable about your product or service makes it very easy for your customers to really understand what your product can do for them.

Examine how Nancy Robinson from Profit Plus Accounting Services completed this workshop.

THE PURPOSE OF THIS WORKSHOP IS (1) TO HELP YOU UNDERSTAND THE DIFFERENCE BETWEEN FEATURES AND BENEFITS (2) TO HELP YOU TRANSLATE YOUR FEATURES INTO BENEFITS AND (3) TO ASSURE THAT YOU SPEAK YOUR CUSTOMERS' LANGUAGE.

Personal Workshop #23
Features vs. Benefits

1. List the features (characteristics) of your product or service.

2. For each feature, list how the customer can benefit from that feature. Note there may be more than one benefit related to each feature. Benefits may differ by market niche.

3. For each market niche you plan to serve, prioritize the benefits you listed above.

Feature	Benefit to Customer	Niche A Priorities	Niche B Priorities	Niche C Priorities
Prepare tax returns	Answer "so what?" from the customer's point of view	Minimizes taxes	No need to understand tax law	
Prepare financial statements	Minimizes taxes Minimizes potential underpayment of taxes, Saves time No need to understand tax law	Lets me look at bottom line	Keeps banker happy	
Prepare management letters	Keeps banker happy Provides great ideas to improve my internal controls Provides great ideas to improve my business.	Provides great ideas to improve my business	Keeps banker happy	

Personal Workshop #23
Features vs. Benefits

1. List the features (characteristics) of your product or service.

2. For each feature, list how the customer can benefit from that feature. Note there may be more than one benefit related to each feature. Benefits may differ by market niche.

3. For each market niche you plan to serve, prioritize the benefits you listed above.

Feature	Benefit to Customer	Niche A Priorities	Niche B Priorities	Niche C Priorities

Workshop Follow-Up

✔ After completing this workshop, you should have a good idea of what the "hot buttons" are for each of the markets you plan to serve. This will be the basis for all your promotional messages. Rather than throwing all of the possible benefits at potential customers and hoping one will hit the spot, you will highlight the most important benefit to the niche you plan to serve. If you are not sure how your customers would prioritize the benefits, now is the time to find out by asking them. Review your notes from Challenge 1 to decide the best way to collect information on your customers' priorities.

Positioning

Positioning is the image or picture you want to paint in your potential customers' minds. Your position gives your customers the reasons why they should buy from you rather than your competition. Positioning starts with a product, service, company, institution, or even a person. Positioning is not what you do to that product or service. Positioning is what you do to the mind of the potential customers. You position the product in the mind of the prospect; therefore, you need to know who your potential customers are and what they want from your product.

The easiest way to get into a person's mind is to be the best. What do people consider as the 'best' watch? A Rolex. Now, what is the second 'best' watch? Who knows?

In order to differentiate your product or service from your competition, you need to decide what you are selling. If the product or service has a unique attribute, let it sell itself. If not, you can position your product on:

• Convenience

• Features

• Service

• Selection

• Price

But you can't do all five and make a profit!

A former nurse and now manufacturer of cloth dolls has been able to produce over $200,000 in annual sales by creating designs that depict handicapped children of different ages, races and afflictions. This is an area that no major toy company had touched.

As you are positioning your product or service, keep in mind that the position you select will be based on how you can serve the needs of your customers better than your competitors can. So determine what attributes are important to your customers. Then evaluate the attributes of your business and see where your competition rates on those attributes. You will not want to go head-to-head with your competition. Instead find a group or "niche" that is not being served, and serve it.

Personal Workshop Preparation #24: Describing Your Niche

Your goal with this workshop is to find segments of the market or niches that your competition either does not serve well or ignores. Use criteria that your customers feel are important in their decision to buy the product or service you offer. Then think about what you want to communicate to each niche based on your special position.

Nancy Robinson of Profit Plus Accounting Services wanted to define her niche. She began by listing her competitors, their strengths and weaknesses, and the characteristics important to clients.

Personal Notes

_____

_____

_____

_____

Levi Strauss experienced a significant slowdown in sales in the 1980s as its male Baby Boomer customers reached their 30s and didn't quite fit into their old jeans any more. To keep the interest of this age group, the company launched a whole new division—Dockers—which combines the sense of reliability of the Levi name with a whole new kind of fit and style. Dockers are jeans that you can wear to work, and after work. They move easily when you move. The Dockers division now does over $1 billion in annual sales and is the only widely recognized brand of pants for men.

THE PURPOSE OF THIS WORKSHOP IS: (1) TO COMPARE YOUR PRODUCT/SERVICE TO THAT OF YOUR COMPETITION (2) DETERMINE WHAT IS IMPORTANT TO YOUR CUSTOMERS AND (3) DETERMINE WHAT YOU WILL COMMUNICATE TO EACH NICHE.

Personal Workshop #24
Describing Your Niche

1. Describe as completely as possible the main products or services that compete for your customer. For example, think not only of direct competitors such as another brand of potato chips, but also of other products that could satisfy a customer's desire to snack, such as pretzels, carrots, or popcorn.

2. Next to each of your major competitors, write a description of its strengths and weaknesses. Strengths could include the features of the product or service, or the benefits that are advertised. Weaknesses include missing features, or features that don't perform as well as yours do. (Look for ads or promotional material, or ask your customers what they think.) **Be sure to use a customer's point of view when you complete this section.**

Competitive Products/Services	Strengths	Weaknesses	Important Characteristics
Accounting Software	Inexpensive Do work in-house	Not flexible Must have understanding of accounting to use	Understanding of accounting
Bookkeeper	Inexpensive Get information needed for tax purposes	Doesn't provide advice Doesn't help set up accounts to provide good management information	Advice
XYZ Accounting	Lots of experts	Expensive Don't pay much attention to smaller clients Don't talk in a language the business owners understand	Advice that is understandable
Smith Accounting	Inexpensive Does tax work, bookkeeping and financial management	Not responsive to clients Often misses deadlines	Responsive

3. Pick the two most important characteristics in the decision to purchase a product or service. Then graph where you and your competitors stand. **Be sure to do this from a customer's point of view.**

High   XYZ
                                                                  Accounting

Average   Profit Plus Accounting

Poor |
          | Smith Accounting
          |_____
          Low   Medium   High

4. Once you have identified the niche or niches that you will fill, describe each niche in one sentence. For example, "The specialist in shoes of small size," or "The freshest produce of any supermarket," or "The restaurant with the most fun-loving waitresses."

The answer for entrepreneurial companies that need an accountant who can serve as a financial manager.

THE PURPOSE OF THIS WORKSHOP IS: (1) TO COMPARE YOUR PRODUCT/SERVICE TO YOUR COMPETITION (2) DETERMINE WHAT IS IMPORTANT TO YOUR CUSTOMERS AND (3) DETERMINE WHAT YOU WILL COMMUNICATE TO EACH NICHE.

Personal Workshop #24
Describing Your Niche

1. Describe as completely as possible the main products or services that compete for your customer. For example, think not only of direct competitors such as another brand of potato chips, but also of other products that could satisfy a customer's desire to snack, such as pretzels, carrots, or popcorn.

2. Next to each of your major competitors, write a description of its strengths and weaknesses. Strengths could include the features of the product or service, or the benefits that are advertised. Weaknesses include missing features, or features that don't perform as well as yours do. (Look for ads or promotional material, or ask your customers what they think.) **Be sure to use a customer's point of view when you complete this section.**

Competitive Products/Services	*Strengths*	*Weaknesses*	*Important Characteristics*

3. Pick the two most important characteristics in the decision to purchase a product or service. Then graph where you and your competitors stand. **Be sure to do this from a customer's point of view.**

4. Once you have identified the niche or niches that you will fill, describe each niche in one sentence. For example, "The specialist in shoes of small size," or "The freshest produce of any supermarket," or "The restaurant with the most fun-loving waitresses."

Workshop Follow-Up

 1. Using the competitive grid produces a visual picture of how your competition is seen by potential customers. It may reveal an opportune position for your company to achieve a unique selling proposition.

 2. Reducing your positioning statement to one or two sentences provides a central theme for all your advertising, sales promotions, and other communications with your market.

 3. A compact positioning statement also makes it easier for your employees and your customers to remember what you would like them to communicate about your product or service.

 Specialization can be scary, because you may feel that by narrowing down your market you may have too few customers to keep your business alive. Once you have defined potential niches, you can go back to the marketing planning section to estimate the market demand for your product or service. If you select a niche that is too small, you may have to build your business niche by niche.

Positioning is based on the simple realization that customers are overwhelmed with information and advertising claims today. Because they are bombarded with promotional messages, they tend to quickly determine whether a product or service may be of benefit to them. If they don't see a benefit, they discard your message.

One reason small businesses fail is that they never find a niche. They never discover and communicate why they are "better and different" than their competition. You have seen these businesses—the neighborhood dry cleaner or restaurant that opened with great fanfare, only to close a year later. Face up to one critical fact: most customers are not waiting for another mediocre business to try to serve them. Today's customers are too smart to give their money to just any business.

Finding the right position is only your first challenge. To turn this unique position into sales, you must be prepared to back it up with a comprehensive marketing plan. Once you have selected your position, more than anything else, successful positioning requires consistency. You must keep at it year after year. Your position is the basis for all your promotional messages. Next you will look at how to actually write the copy or sales pitch.

 Successful consultants average more than $3000 per year per client. If their initial sales goal is $100,000 with a 10 percent growth thereafter, they need 30 to 35 first-year clients with access to five to seven new clients each year. It may be difficult to find enough small business clients who can afford to pay $3000 in a year; therefore, the consultant will need to select another niche, such as medium-sized wholesalers, to create a viable business.

Promotional Copywriting

As you develop the message you want to communicate to your audience, select the style of writing that will work for the niche that you want to communicate with. Don't try to impress your audience with big words or industry jargon. Even if you are writing to PhDs, write your copy at about the eighth-grade level. Direct your message to the people who will buy. Don't worry about writing to the people who will not buy. They have already turned the page, tossed the piece, or tuned out.

Your copy does not have to be hard sell and slick. But it should be exciting, specific, crisp, relevant, and pithy. Your copy should:

- Highlight the product distinctions that are important to the customer

- "Speak with one voice"

- Register the product/service/business name

- Use pictures only if they tell the story

- Signal clearly who is the target

- Be simple

- Gain attention

A good copywriter will see the prospect's interests, his or her angle, and will accommodate a stance for that individual. You need to spend more time thinking about the reader than about what you have to say. Don't tell people what they need to know, tell them what they want to know.

There are a lot of checklists and formulas available for the copywriter to follow. No one formula works best. You will have to adapt the checklist to suit your needs. The simplest formula is actually a sales formula:

A	Get **A**ction
I	Arouse **I**nterest
D	Stimulate **D**esire
A	Ask for **A**ction

Copy Tips

It can be very difficult to begin writing copy. It is hard to come up with ideas when you are staring at a blank screen. Often it is easier to take some of your old copy and begin to modify it. Once you begin writing, write down everything that comes to mind. Don't start to edit your copy as you are writing it. That will stifle

The concept behind positioning is easy to state: find a hole and fill it. Promote the most important benefit, or the two most important benefits, to the niche(s) you have selected.

FYI

your creativity. Instead, get as many ideas down on paper as you can. Later you can go back to edit and modify what you have written.

In the editing process, make sure your copy focuses on benefits to the customer, not features of the product or service. Make sure you focus on the one or two benefits that will be most important to the recipient. By providing a laundry list of benefits, you are communicating to potential customers that you do not know what they want, but you are everything to everyone. By focusing on the benefit most important to potential customers, you will attract their attention.

Make sure the benefit is the center of attention, not the copy. How many times do you remember a clever commercial but have no idea what product it was advertising? Your promotion dollar is too valuable to chance wasting it.

Use questionnaires and quizzes to help readers discover benefits. When listing your benefits, be very specific—generalities don't sell. Tell the reader, listener, or viewer exactly what he or she will get. If you are writing to scientists or engineers, use statistics for proof. If you are writing to sales people or managers, use testimonials for proof.

Very often you will find that the first few paragraphs of a letter are your warm-up. You wrote them to get your mind moving, but they don't really add to your letter. In fact your letter would be stronger if you eliminated them. Check to see if you got right to the point in paragraph one, or whether it could be eliminated to make your copy stronger.

Make your copy look easy to read. Remember, we are not a nation of readers. If it takes effort to read, we won't read it. Keep your paragraphs short, so your copy looks easier to read. Use action verbs. Wherever possible, break up your copy. You can do this with subheads, quotes, testimonials, or checklists. Wherever you have more than two features, benefits, or ideas, use bullets instead of separating with commas.

In your copy, try to develop a one-to-one relationship with the reader. Write as if you are writing to a specific person. It is helpful to have a good customer in mind and write as if you are writing to that individual. Use first person, present tense. Don't depersonalize, for example, by saying "Payment at this time is not required," instead of "Send no money now." Don't be guilty of the *I'm not responsible syndrome*. For example, "You have been selected...".

FYI

Questions Your Copy Should Answer:
1. What is this about?
2. How does it concern me?
3. How can you prove it?
4. What do you want me to do?
5. Why should I do it?

Whether your copy will be heard or read, write the way you speak. Good copy is not always good grammar. If breaking a grammar rule will help you communicate more effectively, do so. For example, sometimes an incomplete sentence will communicate more effectively than a grammatically correct one.

Ask for the response or the order. You may need to repeat the offer three or more times in various manners. Remember, no one reads or listens to your entire message. If your offer is not stated more than once, the prospect may miss it. End by telling the reader what to do, when to do it, how to do it, and what might be lost if he/she doesn't do it.

Types of Copy

Nothing is worse than staring at a blank screen or sheet of paper when you are trying to write copy. Use the following types of copy as idea generators. For example, begin to write questions your customers might ask along with answers. But don't worry about whether that is the best format—just start getting your ideas down.

> *"Kodak sells film but they don't advertise film. They advertise memories."*
>
> —Theodore Levitt

Question and answer (answer the questions honestly)
    Storytelling or narrative?   Patriotic offers?

Testimonials (don't edit them—despite poor grammar, they are more believable)
    Reason why   Description
    Dialogue   Humor

Words to Use

Another way to get your creative juices flowing is to try to use some of the following words to describe the benefits your customers will receive. These words can also be used in the editing stage, to make sure that you are using words that sell. See if you can replace some of the words you have written with the words below.

Act	Hurry	Only	Today
Advantage	Imagine	Opportunity	Unique
Benefit	Invite	Profit	Valuable
Boost	Just arrived	Protect	Value
Build	Know	Proven	Win
Convenient	Last chance	Results	Worth
Delight	Learn	Reward	
Discover	Limited time offer	Save	
Easy	New	Save time	
Exciting	Never before	Satisfaction guaranteed	
Free	No obligation	Secrets	
Fast	Not sold in stores	Send no money now	
Guaranteed	Now you can	Thanks	
How to	Offer expires January 1		

Personal Workshop Preparation #25:
Writing Your Copy

The goal of this workshop is to get you started writing copy. Select three words from the list of "Words to Use" that might be used to describe your product or service. Write a sentence promoting your product/service with each of the words you chose. Feel free to note ideas for graphics or logos that you might want to include.

Jerry Lee from Trade Winds Grocery was unable to come up with any ideas for an ad in the local paper. He decided to choose three words to use in sentences to get his creative juices flowing.

THE PURPOSE OF THIS WORKSHOP IS TO WRITE A SENTENCE PROMOTING YOUR PRODUCT/SERVICE.

Personal Workshop #25

Writing Your Copy

The words I selected to use are:

Just arrived

Imagine

Unique

My promotional copy:

Just arrived, three new flavors of Paradise Potions uniquely flavored dips.

Imagine impressing your guests with the tantalizing taste of fresh seafood and Paradise Potions seafood sauce.

Looking for something unique to serve for dinner? Stop by Trade Winds Grocery.

THE PURPOSE OF THIS WORKSHOP IS TO WRITE A SENTENCE PROMOTING YOUR PRODUCT/SERVICE.

Personal Workshop #25
Writing Your Copy

The words I selected to use are:

My promotional copy:

FYI

Early in my marketing career, I thought I could not write promotions because I was not creative. When my boss asked me to write a promotional letter, I wrote the world's worst. I am sure the sales department said, "There goes the marketing department sending out useless promotions." The letter was poor because it had no specific objective, and I had very little knowledge of why customers bought or the strengths and weaknesses of the competition.

In my next position, I began by conducting focus groups on the videotapes for which I would later write promotional copy. When asked to review the current promotional copy and make suggestions, I learned that I *could* write copy. I just needed to "steal the customer's own words." Sales of the videocassettes jumped from $5,000 per year to $100,000 per year.

–Gloria Green

Workshop Follow-Up

 By getting something down on paper or on the computer, you will get your creative juices flowing. You will have begun to give some thought to the messages that you want to communicate to your market niches. Finally, you will have reviewed the words that sell and selected some that you should be using in your promotional copy.

Headlines

The part of your copy that is read most often is your headline. If you can attract attention with your headline, the reader will begin to read your copy. So be sure your headline:

- attracts attention

- tells who you are talking to

- delivers a complete message

- draws the reader into the body copy

A Headline Should...

...offer a benefit

We can turn your IBM PC into an engineering workstation.

What if you could identify, segment, target, and sell your prospects and customers so precisely that you cut your present marketing costs by 67% and increased your sales by 52%?

...make a promise

Don't pay a penny for repairs, belts, hoses or oil—for three years.

...identify the prospect

I never bought stocks before—how do I go about it?

...give news

Look at what you get in the new Oxbridge Directory of Newsletters.

Introducing the Xerox 1020 copier, the smallest copier in our impressive new marathon series.

 You are both a writer and an editor when you write copy. But be careful! When you begin writing copy, allow creativity to flow. Editing your copy too early may cause your creative juices to stop flowing. Force yourself to write down all of your ideas before you begin the editing process. Writing and editing need to be two different steps. Often it is best to separate these two steps by a day.

...identify a problem

Ineffective employees cost you money.

Why struggle with a big tiller?

Probably one of the toughest problems either you or I will ever have to face is retirement.

...make an offer

An invitation to save money.

After high school, there should be more than nine to five... There should be a little bit of adventure.

When I deal with print production, these two practical books save me time, money, and hassle.

...tell a story

They laughed when I sat down at the piano.

The best manager I ever hired ... $19,000 for life.

Dad told me, "Joe, always give the customers a little more than they pay for."

Personal Workshop Preparation #26: Headlines

The goal of this workshop is to review headlines to see if you can make them more effective.

Ads from Trade Winds Grocer and Profit Plus Accounting Services are shown as examples. You will find it is easier to critique someone else's headlines than your own. Once you see their mistakes, you are less likely to make the same mistake. So begin by analyzing the headlines for the ads shown.

I n a direct mail letter, your headline is the P.S. When people look to see who sent the letter, their eye is automatically drawn to the P.S. (We were all taught to read left to right and up to down, so our eye naturally goes from the signature to the P.S.) If you catch your readers' interest with the P.S., they will begin to read the letter.

FYI

THE PURPOSE OF THIS WORKSHOP IS TO LEARN TO DETERMINE WHETHER A HEADLINE ATTRACTS ATTENTION; DETERMINE WHETHER A HEADLINE SPEAKS TO A SPECIFIC NICHE; DETERMINE WHETHER A HEADLINE DELIVERS A COMPLETE MESSAGE; DETERMINE WHETHER A HEADLINE GOES WITH THE AD

Personal Workshop #26

Headlines

Large Selection of Asian, South American and Caribbean Foods

Salsa	Bulkoki
Barbeque Sauce	Kalbi
Spices	Fahitas
Seafood Sauce	Choriso
Egg Rolls	Sweet Breads
Sashimi	Mexican Spices

Trade Winds Grocery
255-2525

Is the headline clear?

Yes, the headline is clear, but very feature oriented.

Does it communicate the benefit?

No, only the feature of large selection and the types of food are communicated.

Does it speak to your most likely customers?

Yes, it does speak to people interested in those cuisines.

Is it interesting?

Not really. It does not make anyone want to go out of their way to shop at Trade Winds.

Can it be made more specific?

Yes, it could be made more specific. Could be targeted toward gourmet cooks, one specific cuisine, party dishes, hor d'oeuvres, main dishes, or desserts.

Does it work with the visual?

Not really, the visual shows a grocery basket of foods that are not necessarily Asian, South American or Caribbean.

THE PURPOSE OF THIS WORKSHOP IS TO LEARN TO DETERMINE WHETHER A HEADLINE ATTRACTS ATTENTION; DETERMINE WHETHER A HEADLINE SPEAKS TO A SPECIFIC NICHE; DETERMINE WHETHER A HEADLINE DELIVERS A COMPLETE MESSAGE; DETERMINE WHETHER A HEADLINE GOES WITH THE AD.

Personal Workshop #26

Headlines

---

en.tre.pre.neur

**Someone
Profits Plus Accounting
understands very well.**

And why not. We're entrepreneurs ourselves. It's the reason we are dedicated to serving business owners. And because we understand entrpreneurs so well, we are able to provide solutions.

Profits Plus Accounting
123 Accounting Ave
Anytown, WI 53555
833-8383

Is the headline clear?

No, the headline is not really clear. It is trying to be clever to attract attention. The dictionary phonetic spelling makes it difficult to read. The other problem is that many small business owners do not call themselves entrepreneurs.

Does it communicate the benefit?

In a round about way, the two headings are trying to communicate the benefit.

Does it speak to your most likely customers?

Yes, it does speak to the most likely customers, if they consider themselves entrepreneurs. Simply asking a couple of current clients if they consider themselves an entrepreneur would answer this question.

Is it interesting?

Yes, it is interesting.

Can it be made more specific?

Possibly. For example, "Profit Plus Accounting: Advice You Can Count On for Growing Your Business."

THE PURPOSE OF THIS WORKSHOP IS TO LEARN TO DETERMINE WHETHER A HEADLINE ATTRACTS ATTENTION; DETERMINE WHETHER A HEADLINE SPEAKS TO A SPECIFIC NICHE; DETERMINE WHETHER A HEADLINE DELIVERS A COMPLETE MESSAGE; DETERMINE WHETHER A HEADLINE GOES WITH THE AD.

Personal Workshop #26
Headlines

How would you answer the following questions about headlines you have used? As you answer, think about ways to modify the headline, or to create a new headline that would be more effective. If you don't have headlines that you have used, critique those of your competition.

Place your headline idea here:

Is the headline clear?

Does it communicate the benefit?

Does it speak to your most likely customers?

Is it interesting?

Can it be made more specific?

Does it work with the visual?

Workshop Follow-Up

By critiquing headlines that you have used in the past, you will quit making the same mistakes. By critiquing your competitors' headlines, you will learn from their mistakes. Through the process of critiquing, you will develop stronger headlines that attract attention and communicate your message.

Personal Workshop Preparation #27: Checklist for Print Promotion

Your goal with this workshop is to evaluate your advertisements, direct mail pieces, sales materials, and sales promotional materials. You will be looking for ways to improve your written communication with customers and potential customers. Think about how you may need to change your printed pieces as you answer the following questions.

As a preview of this workshop, take a look at how Jerry Lee from Trade Winds Grocery and Nancy Robinson from Profits Plus Accounting Services completed this workshop.

Finally, a Tip from an Anonymous Expert

FYI

Probably the most often quoted advice on advertising copywriting is in the form of a poem written many years ago by a now forgotten author.

I see that you've spent quite a big wad of dough
    To tell me the things you think I should know.
How your plant is so big, so fine and strong;
    And your founder has whiskers so handsomely long.

So he started the business in old '92?
    How tremendously int'resting that is—to you.
He built up the thing with the blood of his life?
    (I'll run home like mad, tell that to my wife!)

Your machinery's modern and, oh, so complete!
    Your "rep" is so flawless; your workers so neat.
Your motto is "Quality"—capital "Q,"
    No wonder I'm tired of "your" and "you"!

So tell me quick and tell me true
    (Or else my love, to hell with you!)
Less—"how this product came to be";
    More—what the damn thing does for me!

THE PURPOSE OF THIS WORKSHOP IS TO OBJECTIVELY REVIEW AND EDIT YOUR PROMOTIONAL MATERIALS TO SPOT WEAKNESSES IN YOUR PROMOTIONS AND TO CREATE PROMOTIONS THAT COMMUNICATE EFFECTIVELY

Personal Workshop #27
Checklist for Print Promotion

Large Selection of Asian, South American and Caribbean Foods

Salsa	Bulkoki
Barbeque Sauce	Kalbi
Spices	Fahitas
Seafood Sauce	Choriso
Egg Rolls	Sweet Breads
Sashimi	Mexican Spices

Trade Winds Grocery
255-2525

Is it written as you speak?

Yes, the copy is written as I would say it.

How many points does it attempt to make?

It attempts to make one point—that we carry a large selection of foods.

How many products/services/promotions are emphasized?

It tries to convey all the different products that the store carries in the hope that at least one will be interesting enough to draw customers into the store. It might be stronger if a cooking demonstration was promoted. Then once customers are in the store for the demonstration, the visual merchandising of the store would communicate the range of products sold.

Does the headline communicate your message?

Yes, the headline communicates the message.

Do you talk to a specific market or all markets?

It does not talk to a specific market. The headline could be geared to gourmet cooks, people planning graduation parties, or people with an interest in a particular cuisine.

Does the ad visually say what the wording says?

No, the food basket does not necessarily say Asian, South American or Caribbean foods.

Did you BAF the reader: start with benefits, then advantages, then features?

No benefits are mentioned in the ad. The ad focuses on the features, the particular products we sell. A benefit-oriented headline might read "Get out of the same old meal doldrums."

Are you selling specifics, not generalities?

Trade Winds is selling generic product categories. By promoting particular brand names, we may be able to obtain cooperative advertising dollars. By advertising hard-to-find brands, we will attract attention of the people who like that particular product.

Could a competitor put his/her name on your ad and run it?

Yes, any grocery store could use this ad. It does not distinguish the store from other stores.

What could be eliminated to make it more effective?

Eliminate the long list of food products we carry. Eliminate the visual as it does not really aid in communication.

Can you divide the copy up with subheads that sell?

There really is not enough copy to divide up.

Does the layout help draw the reader into the ad?

Somewhat.

Does the copy help the promotion to do what you want it to: generate leads, sell the product, qualify leads, etc.?

No, the copy does not suggest that people come into the store. We list the store name and the phone number, but we don't really want people to call. To get people to come into the store, we should include the address, directions if necessary, and the store hours.

Did you ask for the order or the inquiry?

No, we did not ask people to stop by the store. That could be done by saying "Stop in Monday through Friday 10 AM to 8 PM or Saturday 10 AM to 6 PM."

Did you include your name, phone number and address on every piece in the package?

The name and phone number were included, but the address was missing.

THE PURPOSE OF THIS WORKSHOP IS TO OBJECTIVELY REVIEW AND EDIT YOUR PROMOTIONAL MATERIALS TO SPOT WEAKNESSES IN YOUR PROMOTIONS AND TO CREATE PROMOTIONS THAT COMMUNICATE EFFECTIVELY

Personal Workshop #27
Checklist for Print Promotion

en.tre.pre.neur

**Someone
Profits Plus Accounting
understands very well.**

And why not. We're entrepreneurs ourselves. It's the reason we are dedicated to serving business owners. And because we understand entrepreneurs so well, we are able to provide solutions.

Profits Plus Accounting
123 Accounting Ave
Anytown, WI 53555
833-8383

Is it written as you speak?

The headline is difficult to read because we used the phonetic spelling. The copy is written as spoken.

How many points does it attempt to make?

The ad attempts to make one point, that Profit Plus understands and serves entrepreneurs.

How many products/services/promotions are emphasized?

It emphasizes that we serve entrepreneurs. Other than the name Profit Plus Accounting, we really don't tell what services are available.

Does the headline communicate your message?

The headline communicates that we understand entrepreneurs, but it does not tell how a client would benefit from this understanding.

Do you talk to a specific market or all markets?

It does talk to a specific market.

Did you BAF the reader: start with benefits, then advantages, then features?

We tried to communicate the benefit, but did not go quite far enough. We went past the feature of offering accounting services to say that we understand entrepreneurs. But the only clue as to why a potential client would benefit was that because we understand entrepreneurs, we can provide solutions.

Are you selling specifics, not generalities?

We are selling our general knowledge of understanding entrepreneurs. To make it more specific we could say, "Profit Plus Accounting: Your On-Call Controller."

Could a competitor put his/her name on your ad and run it?

Any local accounting firm and even national accounting firms could use this ad. It tries to distinguish them from accountants who just crunch numbers. But it does not distinguish them from all the other accountants who say they do more than crunch numbers.

What could be eliminated to make it more effective?

The phonetic spelling of entrepreneurs. Also the address. We don't really want people to stop by.

Can you divide the copy up with subheads that sell?

With the amount of copy in this ad, the single subhead that is used is probably enough.

Does the layout help draw the reader into the ad?

The layout is not very exciting. But the headline may catch the attention of people who consider themselves entrepreneurs.

Does the copy help the promotion to do what you want it to: generate leads, sell the product, qualify leads, etc.?

The copy only creates an image in the mind of the reader. It does not suggest any kind of action.

Did you ask for the order or the inquiry?

No, we did not ask for the client to call or even to consider Profit Plus for their accounting needs.

Did you include your name, phone number and address on every piece in the package?

We did include the name, address and phone number. But in this case, the address is probably not necessary. Most accounting firms can not handle walk in business, so we want to discourage it.

THE PURPOSE OF THIS WORKSHOP IS TO OBJECTIVELY REVIEW AND EDIT YOUR PROMOTIONAL MATERIALS TO SPOT WEAKNESSES IN YOUR PROMOTIONS AND TO CREATE PROMOTIONS THAT COMMUNICATE EFFECTIVELY.

Personal Workshop #27
Checklist For Print Promotion

Answer each of the following questions as honestly as possible. Then edit your copy until you are satisfied with the answers to these questions.

Is it written as you speak?

How many points does it attempt to make?

How many products/services/promotions are emphasized?

Does the headline communicate your message?

Do you talk to a specific market or all markets?

Does the ad visually say what the wording says?

Did you BAF the reader: start with benefits, then advantages, then features?

Are you selling specifics, not generalities?

Could a competitor put his/her name on your ad and run it?

What could be eliminated to make it more effective?

Can you divide the copy up with subheads that sell?

Does the layout help draw the reader into the ad?

Does the copy help the promotion to do what you want it to: generate leads, sell the product, qualify leads, etc.?

Did you ask for the order or the inquiry?

Did you include your name, phone number and address on every piece in the package?

Place your edited ad copy here. Share your copy with your employees. What are their responses to the ad?

Workshop Follow-Up

By critiquing your ads and promotional pieces, you will develop better promotions. You will make sure that you are:

- communicating the message that you want to communicate
- designing the promotion to do what you want it to do
- asking for some action, either an inquiry or a sale
- including the information your prospect needs to make a decision

How Messages are Communicated

Promotional messages are communicated through some blend of the promotional tools which include:

- Word-of-Mouth, Networking, Personal Referrals
- Direct Mail

- Personal Selling
- Telemarketing
- Public Relations

- Sales Promotions
- Advertising
- Merchandising

Word-of-Mouth, Networking, Personal Referrals

The key to the success of this promotional tool is to underpromise and overdeliver. Positive talk begins when you consistently exceed customers' expectations. Word-of-mouth marketing ultimately depends on the quality of your customer service. The talk about your business outside your business often reflects your insider talk—what your employees say about you. Listen to your insider talk, the talk inside your own company about your company, and reward those who talk positively.

Develop a relationship with your customers, find out their wants and needs, and solicit their complaints. One way to get your clients involved is by participating in a focus group, or asking for their advice. Make it easy for your customers to complain: ask for their complaints. Then act on the information you receive from your customers. If you don't act, your customers will quit providing you with complaints, and complaints are your opportunity to satisfy an unhappy customer.

> *"Salesmen must act as if they are on the customer's payroll."*
>
> —Buck Rodgers

Everyone gets some referrals from satisfied customers without even asking. But very few businesses have procedures for encouraging referrals from their current customers, their prospects, their friends, and people they meet in social or business settings. The key is to determine who your champions are, identify their networks, identify ways they can help you, make it easy for them to help you, and reward them for helping you. Start by asking your satisfied customers for testimonials. Then ask who else they know who needs your product or service.

Networking is the art of getting what you want through other people. It is not attending business card exchanges or belonging to associations or chambers in name only. It is developing relationships with people who are in your niche, or people who will refer a niche to you.

Develop some outrageous ideas to start people talking. Use the idea to get attention, then sell your product on its benefits. Table 3.3 displays ideas to get you started actively soliciting word-of-mouth or referrals.

FYI

A meeting planner was networking with a women's entrepreneur group. She was active on committees, and even planned its events. When asked how many of the members were in her target market, her mouth fell to the floor. None of the businesses were large enough to hold meetings that might require her services. All the marketing she thought she was doing had not brought her a single client.

Table 3.3: Word-of-Mouth Ideas

Do one little thing, free of charge.

Assemble a goof kit, a small gift to give to your customers when you make a mistake.

Have business cards for every employee to pass out to prospects and customers.

Contact all customers after they do business to find out if they were satisfied, ask them to do business again, and ask them to tell their friends.

Display any press, complimentary letters from customers, awards, etc. where your customers can see them.

Create heroes in your business. Whenever an employee does something outstanding, celebrate it.

Don't assume; find out by asking.

Send a special gift to employees' families when they have to go out of town or work extra hours.

Make a family day, a day for employees' families to visit your business.

Establish a customer advisory board.

Learn and use your customers' names.

Extend your hours to meet your customers' needs, not to fit your needs.

Give a treat to the children, after asking the parents' permission, of course.

Turn your customers into VIPs. Have special sales or promotions for them.

If you can't fill a customer's request, send him or her to the competition.

Take pictures of customers buying big ticket items and place them on a bulletin board.

Show your appreciation for your customer's business, with a simple thank you, a note, or a token of your appreciation.

Offer tours of your business.

Allow customers to test products right in your store.

Do little things for customers as a matter of policy.

Enrich somebody's mind instead of their belly, send novels instead of food or candy as a gift.

Answer an inquiry with an audio tape instead of a letter.

Sometimes customers are reluctant to provide referrals because they are afraid you will hound their friends. When you ask for referrals, explain exactly what you plan to do: send a letter, call, etc. You may need to give your word that you will only follow up if the friend expresses an interest.

 FYI

Direct Mail, Personal Letters, Flyers

Direct mail is often considered junk mail. That is because most of it is junk. Think about a direct mail piece that you received in the last week that you considered junk. Now think about a direct mail piece you received in the last month that was not junk. What was the difference between those two pieces?

You probably did not answer that one was four color, or that it had a fancy pop-out. The answer was that it offered something of interest to you. So the key to success in direct mail is to send your offer only to those who are interested. That means finding the best mailing list.

Now think about the last direct mail piece you developed. How much time did you spend writing and editing the copy? How much time did you spend on developing the layout, selecting the paper, and getting the piece ready for the printer? How much time did you spend selecting the mailing list?

Most people spend five to twenty hours on the copy and about the same amount of time on the layout. But they spend about five minutes on the list. Often the thought process is "We need a count for the printer. Which mailing list should we use?" Then a secretary is told to get a mailing list. Why does everyone receive so much junk mail? Because the most important decision in direct mail, the list, is basically ignored.

As with all promotional tools, direct mail can be used to sell direct, generate leads, qualify leads, reinforce selling, or create awareness. Often the expectations of what direct mail can do are incorrect. Many business owners who are uncomfortable with selling try to use direct mail instead. Direct mail can not directly sell services or highly complex products. It can qualify leads to be followed up with personal selling. A mailing piece designed to qualify leads will not tell the whole story. It will only generate interest and leave the storytelling to the salesperson. If your mailing piece tells the whole story, it leaves no questions unanswered.

Profit Plus Accounting, Nancy Robinson: I sent out a mailing to generate some new clients. In the mailing I included a complete description of the services I offer and my bio. I got no response to my mailing so I concluded that direct mail did not work.

A marketing consultant suggested that I use direct mail to try to generate some leads, rather than making cold calls. I sent out a mailing that established my credibility and offered a free guide to managing cash flow. I obtained some leads from this mailing, and so far I have converted one into a new client.

Don't try to use direct mail without...

1. A clearly defined market of wants or needs. You must have an absolutely clear understanding of the problems your prospects have.

2. A product or service that satisfies that want or need. You must understand how your product or service will help prospects solve their problems and what benefits they will gain by using your product or service.

3. A list that truly represents the market, or at least a segment of it. You need to develop a target list of the people who really need your product so you can mail to them over and over until they buy.

4. An attractive offer to make. Your copy should stress the benefits to be derived from using your product or service and the need to take action NOW to secure these benefits.

The List

Internal or In-house Lists

Obviously, the best list that you can use is a list of your past customers. If you do not have a list of past customers, now is the time to start putting one together. It is difficult, costly, and sometimes impossible to reconstruct mailing lists that were not retained at the time they became available. You will have to make the cost vs. benefit decision on whether to try to reconstruct the mailing list of your prior customers.

External Lists

The information you gather from your in-house list can be utilized to help you select outside or external lists. There are four basic types of external lists:

Responder Lists: people who have bought by mail from someone else are usually the best prospects to buy again.

Compiled Lists: names and addresses of people and organizations who are qualified to be on the list.

Magazine Lists: people who subscribe to a particular magazine can be in a cross-section between a responder list (they probably bought the magazine subscription through the mail), and a compiled list (they may not purchase other items through the mail).

Association Lists: people who belong to a particular association are frequently the most overlooked.

The mailing list you use, or the people to whom you distribute flyers will have more impact on the success of a direct mail campaign than the copy you write or the piece you design.

FYI

The Package

The items you use to send your offer to your audience are called the package. The package is the look of the direct mailing. For maximum results, always think of a mailing unit as a package—with all of the elements working together. The package can range from being a simple self-mailer to an envelope filled with a variety of items.

Within the package you must have:

1. An offer

2. Information the prospect needs to make a decision

3. A response vehicle

A heavier emphasis is placed on personal letters, flyers and direct mail when:

• the target market can be narrowly defined

• the product is not highly complex or technical

• the product or service is purchased frequently

• you have more than one target market with varying needs

Personal Selling

If you are a small business owner, you are a salesperson. Selling does not mean pushing your product or service on your customers, it means listening to and trying to satisfy the needs of the customers. If your product or service really will fulfill the customers' needs better than that of your competition, you are doing customers a favor by letting them know. If you have not bothered to qualify your customers, you are interrupting them.

Schedule some time every day for selling, and be sure it is during selling hours. Too often businesses find themselves in the feast or famine cycle. They sell only when they have no work. Then they spend eight hours a day selling. As soon as work comes in the door, they quit selling and start producing. When they complete the orders or projects, they have no work, so they are back to selling eight hours a day.

Don't always assume that the first "no" means "no." Find out what the true objection is and determine how you can best meet their needs. If you don't, your competitor will. If you have done a good job in qualifying the prospect, "no" often means that the customer does not understand how he or she will benefit by purchasing your product or service. Consider an objection an invitation to uncover customer needs and offer a solution.

Most lists are rented for one-time use. List owners seed (put phony names on list) to monitor the use of the list. List owners will prosecute business owners who use their list without authorization.

When the customer has made it clear that he or she will not buy your product or service, get out of the selling mode and into the research mode to find out why. This will provide you with valuable information for future sales calls, and also a foot in the door to this customer in the future.

If you make sales calls empty-handed, you will come out the same way. Line up your sales presentation materials in the order that you will probably use them during the call and tailor them to the specific presentation you will be making. Don't forget to ask for the order. Many sales people sell the product, and then buy it back because they never ask for the sale. Practice asking for the order until you become comfortable with the words you will use.

Steps to Effective Customer-Oriented Selling

Generating Sales Leads

There are many sources for sales leads. The best leads often come from referrals or from your network. Once you have tapped those leads, it is time to look for more. The better the job you have done defining your target market or niche, the easier it will be to determine where to find leads. One source of leads is to read the business news section of your local newspaper. Every time you see someone hired or promoted to a position that has purchasing authority for your product or service, send them a congratulatory letter and follow up on that lead. There are a variety of sources for finding leads in the reference section of your library.

Another source for leads is the yellow pages. Once you have defined your niche, you can look in the yellow pages for a listing of companies. The problem with using the yellow pages is that you find the company name, but not the correct person's name, so you may prefer to use chamber of commerce or other association listings.

Another source is published directories. Most every state has a directory of manufacturers and a directory of services which you will find in the reference section of major libraries.

You can also purchase leads by purchasing a mailing/telemarketing list for unlimited use for a year. To find the list, call a mail list broker. They are listed in the yellow pages under mailing lists. Remember to define your niche as specifically as possible and ask them for list options, so you are making the

FYI

To find a mailing list, look in the yellow pages under mailing lists. There you will find the names of list brokers who can help you find and rent a list. Don't make the mistake many business owners make and let the list broker make your list decision. Instead, ask the list broker for three to five suggestions for your mailing list. Then you make the decision.

list decision. You may decide the list is too large to follow up with every lead. In that case, you may use direct mail or telemarketing to qualify the names on the list.

Another source of leads can be the inquiries that your advertising generates. Often prospects call in for more information. Sometimes your staff is so efficient that they type the name and address directly on the envelope or mailing piece. Once it is mailed, the name is lost.

Ask your suppliers for leads; they have a vested interest in your success. The more you sell, the more they sell. Ask other businesses who serve your niche, but don't compete with you, for leads. Ask your professional advisors for leads. Join a leads group.

Another way to obtain leads is to display at a trade show or convention. If you use this method, be sure you design a program to qualify the leads you obtain. Often sales people will follow up on the first ten or so leads generated by a trade show. If those leads are not good, they won't follow up on the rest. So if you can't qualify the leads at a trade show, use telemarketing or direct mail to qualify the leads before turning them over to the sales force.

Another source of leads is past customers. Continually watch for customers who have not bought in a certain period of time. Follow up with them before they become lost customers.

Qualifying the Prospect

It makes no sense to spend time with prospects who are not in the market for your product or service, or who don't have the authority or purchasing power to buy your product or service. So once you have generated leads, you need to qualify them. This will assure that your sales force (which may consist of just you), focuses its efforts on your most likely customers. To qualify potential prospects, ask the following questions.

• What type of product do you currently use?

• How much of the product do you currently use?

• How much are you currently paying for the product?

FYI

You come into contact with possible leads every day. But often business owners don't even recognize them as leads. If you will look in your middle desk drawer, you will find some untapped leads, probably wrapped in a rubber band. It is the business cards that you have collected over time. Often you attend a business function, obtain some business cards, and then put them in your drawer. By the time you get to following up, you don't remember where you met the person, or what his or her interest might be. So be sure to write notes on the back of each business card before you put it in your drawer. Or better yet, add the name to your mailing list or contact management system.

- How do you use the product?
- How is the purchasing decision made in your company?
- Who makes the purchasing decision?
- What is the biggest problem in running your business?

Gaining Access and Setting the Stage

Once you have qualified the prospects, your goal is to obtain an appointment. Most appointments are set up by phone. The key here is to sell the appointment on the phone, not the product or service. If you provide information on your product or service and answer your prospects' questions over the phone, they feel no need to meet with you. They already have the information they think they need. So don't get trapped into selling the product or service over the phone. Instead suggest that you would like to meet so you can show them the answer to their question. Then be sure to use visuals in your sales presentation.

Gather as much information about the prospects' needs as possible before the appointment. This way you can tailor your presentation. Nothing turns a potential customer off more than a canned sales pitch. That communicates that you know nothing about the prospect; you just want to sell to them. No one cares how much you know until they know how much you care. Show your prospects you care by taking the time to listen to them and to gather additional information about them.

At the appointment, open up and cheer up, and make a complimentary comment. By looking at his or her office, and paying attention to initial comments, assess the personality style of your prospect. Determine whether you should spend time with pleasantries or get right down to business. Based on your approach, the prospect will, in 30 seconds or less, decide whether you can be trusted and are of interest. You only have one chance to make a good first impression, so be prepared to make the best impression you can in the first 30 seconds.

Making the Sales Presentation

Know in advance what you want to say. How many times have you just winged a sales presentation and left wishing you had discussed a few key points that you

FYI

missed? Focus on the information to be relayed and the order in which it should be presented. Don't rehearse the exact words you will say. And be ready to modify your presentation based on the interest of the prospect.

Keep your presentation short. Make your point, illustrate it in the most effective way, and ask for the sale. Don't get in the habit of telling and selling. Instead, encourage your prospect to participate in your discussion. Be sure to really listen to your prospect and modify your presentation based on his or her concerns. Don't interrupt. Let the prospect finish speaking, even if he or she is wrong. Then use questions to correct the misunderstanding. Be interruptible; the more you get the prospect to talk, the more likely you are to obtain the sale.

Don't sell barehanded. Have the appropriate sales promotional materials with you. It is often said that if you go into a sales call empty-handed, you will leave that way. Visually provide evidence or proof through testimonials, statistics or demonstrations.

Stress benefits, not features, and match them to your prospects' needs. Be sure to tell your prospects first what the product does for them, then what features it has which show it will do what you said. Be sure to begin your presentation telling prospects what they want to know, then later you can tell them what you want them to know.

Have a positive attitude. Go in with the assumption that you will sell this prospect. Eliminate phrases that convey uncertainty, such as "maybe I can." If you are not sure, you may put some questions into your prospect's mind.

Managing Objections/Resistance

Handling objections is the most difficult part of the sales process, mainly because of the way the salesperson reacts. When salespeople hear an objection, they often become defensive, therefore they do not listen to and analyze the objection before answering it. Treat all objections with respect. Make sure you stay calm, cool and pleasant.

Turn the objection into a question. Often the first customer's objection is not the real objection. It is just the first thought that came to mind. Other times the objection is simply a put off. You will need to clarify to determine what

FYI

A sales person was demonstrating some marketing software. She had obviously prepared for the presentation. She knew exactly the order in which she wanted to show the software's features. The problem was that her prospect had specific questions that he wanted answered; he did not want to see the standard features that each software package had. Unfortunately, she did not know the software well enough to be able to scrap her pitch and just answer his questions. Since she could not show him how the software could do what he wanted, he determined that it could not. He also became concerned about the technical help that would be available if he were to purchase the software.

the real problem is. Turning the objection into a question allows you to improve your understanding of the customer's needs and wants. As an example, if someone states that the windows you are selling are too expensive, you could turn that objection into the question: "Are you looking for a less expensive window?" From the customer's response, you will then have the opportunity to share the features and benefits of *your* product to the customer. As you can see objections should be welcomed, because you can turn them around into a reason for buying.

Never argue with the prospect. Remember, we do not live by reality, but by our perception of reality. Once you begin to argue, the prospect quits listening and communication is cut off. Use cushions when answering an objection, such as "You are wise to be concerned about that..." Make sure your answer is brief and to the point. But be sure to include a sales point in your answer.

Closing the Sale

Be sure to ask for the sale. Develop a number of different ways to ask for the order or the project. One way is to simply ask "How would you like to proceed?" Another way may be to suggest two alternatives and let the customer choose. Any book on selling will provide you with a plethora of ideas on ways to close a sale. The key is to prepare some in advance of your sales call and to use them. Often it helps to have a closing tool, such as a prepared order form, or a proposal.

Then quit talking after you have asked for the sale. The silence may be uncomfortable, but your prospect may need a moment to think. If you ask for the order and then jump back into your sales pitch, you will need to ask for the order again. Be sure to give your prospect time to respond.

Follow-Up and Customer Satisfaction

The sale is not complete until the customer has the product/service and has paid for it. So don't forget about follow-up. This includes keeping the customer informed of progress and letting the customer know if delivery will be late. Don't just allow your customers to complain to you; solicit their complaints. By handling their complaints, or at least listening to them, you will gain a loyal following.

Write thank you letters to customers. Send them additional product literature so they remain happy with the decision they made. Call them after they have received the

---

When you begin describing the features of your product or service, customers feel like they are being sold, so they automatically put up their defenses: "He is not going to sell me something I don't need." This means they have quit listening. When you begin to describe how the customer benefits, they begin asking questions because they want to learn more.

FYI

product or service to make sure they are happy. Then use this opportunity to make additional sales, gather valuable market information, or ask for referrals.

A heavier emphasis is placed on personal selling when:

*   product is very expensive

*   product is new, unfamiliar, difficult to understand, or complex

*   customer is buying for an organization or resale

*   a purchase contract is involved

*   product is a commodity used in production of other products

*   product is an important professional or personal service such as a lawyer or consultant

*   product has a very high-service aspect such as the installation of a computer software system

*   purchase decision is made by a group

Telemarketing

Telemarketing is a sales approach conducted entirely by phone. It can be selling to customers who call, or calling potential customers. Although telemarketing to consumers is considered a nuisance, it is very useful in business to business marketing. It may take only five minutes to qualify a lead over the phone, while it may take two hours to qualify a lead during a cold call.

In any outbound telemarketing program, your objective can be to sell your product, to sell an appointment, or to keep in contact with current customers. If you are trying to set up appointments, don't get trapped into selling your product by phone. Each time the prospect asks a product or service-related question, you will say, "It is difficult for me to show you over the phone. Would you like to get together on Monday so I can show you?" If you sell the product over the phone, the prospect has no reason to set up an appointment.

Telemarketing is really selling using the telephone. So prepare for a telemarketing call the same way you would prepare for a personal sales call. Plan in advance what questions you would like to ask the prospect in order to determine the need

Actually telemarketers have an advantage over salespeople. They can have a cheat sheet by the phone. Often the cheat sheet is a notebook. It begins with the qualifying questions to ask the prospect. Then based on the answer to the question, it directs the telemarketer to the presentation best suited to the prospect. Next, it includes a section with all the objections a prospect may have along with suggestions on how to handle those objections. Finally, it lists possible ways to close or ask for the order.

for your product or service, make a list of the key benefits you would like to present, and determine how you will close the sale.

Organize time each day to make your phone calls rather than setting aside one day each week. It is difficult for anyone to do telemarketing for more than a couple of hours at a time. Pick the time of day that will be most convenient to your customers, not the time of day most convenient to you.

Follow up with a letter, promotional material or whatever you promised.

Outbound Telemarketing

Outbound telemarketing is a cost effective way to reach your business, industrial or institutional customers. Before implementing an outbound telemarketing campaign, determine which of the following is your objective:

1. Selling directly over the phone, whether it be account cultivation and maintenance, order taking, upgrading, reactivating stagnant accounts, renewals, etc.

2. A lead qualification program to screen and classify leads as immediate prospects, not prospects, or future phone or mail contacts.

3. A follow-up campaign to complement your direct mail marketing efforts. This will make your direct mail program ten times more effective.

4. Selling sales appointments over the phone. You should not get into selling the product, just the appointment.

5. Follow-up on sales to ensure the customer satisfaction.

The steps involved in setting up a telemarketing campaign include determining who to call and what message you want to communicate. See the direct marketing section for more details on selecting a list and making an offer.

Inbound Telemarketing

All businesses must field telephone calls from customers or potential customers. How these calls are handled will impact the image your customers have of your business. Often customers are made to feel that they are an interruption rather than a welcome call. If you do not have a formalized telemarketing operation (even if you don't call it telemarketing), someone has to handle those calls. Look at your telephone system to be sure you are providing your customers with the service they deserve and your potential customers with the information they need to help them buy from you. There are three basic purposes of inbound telemarketing:

1. Providing information about your products, where to buy them, how to assemble them and how to use them.

2. Ordertaking, especially in conjunction with direct mail or other promotions.

3. Encouraging customers to air their complaints by having a customer service number.

Public Relations

Public relations is the management of the image your different publics have of your business. Your different publics include your customers, your suppliers, your advisors, the business community, and the general public. Public relations efforts include press releases, news conferences, sponsorships, donations, informational articles, media talk shows, workshops, seminars, newsletters and educational booklets.

When sending a press release or a letter trying to solicit a feature article, start with the idea or angle that will interest the readers of that publication or listeners or viewers of that station. This means you will have to read the publications or watch or listen to that station to understand what angle will be of interest to them. Do your homework and determine what information the writer or editor may request and have it available. This may include background information, photos, people to interview, statistics, etc. Sending the same generic press release to many publications and stations is often like sending junk mail.

Another way to improve your company's image in the community is to get involved in local organizations and serve on their boards. Or use the experts in your company to gain exposure by offering seminars, appearing on talk shows, or writing informational articles.

Newsletters

Newsletters can be used to build awareness, expand a customer base, encourage repeat business, introduce new products or help position your company. But only if you do them right. Many newsletters get placed in the circular file, or the "I'll-get-to-it-someday pile." Why? Because they are boring, self-congratulatory or poor quality.

To be sure you do your newsletter right:

FYI

> The developer of a product was interested in obtaining some press in magazines to promote his product. He sent a press release to about 50 different magazines and obtained no results. Upon a recommendation, he went to the library, actually read the magazines he wanted press in, determined which editor was most likely to be interested in his product, and wrote a feature story that would be of interest to the readers of that magazine, which just happened to mention his product. Upon sending this information, editors began calling him to discuss the topic. His newest problem was how to get the editors off the phone with him. And his efforts resulted in a number of feature articles in major publications about his product.

1. Start by setting a goal for the newsletter. A newsletter that is designed to build awareness would be written very differently from one designed to encourage repeat business.

2. Determine who you are writing to. If you don't know who you are writing the newsletter for, you can't possibly know their information needs.

3. Provide information, don't just sell your product. Newsletters that are simply an advertisement for your company often don't get read. The reader wants different information than would be found in your sales literature.

4. Keep it simple and inexpensive. The premiere issue of your newsletter should approximate what your future issues will look like. If you go all out on the first issue, chances are that it will be too much work or too expensive to do on a regular basis.

5. Develop a system for collecting information for your newsletter. You will need a constant supply of information that is of interest to the reader. It may come from trade journals, questions customers have, articles on customers, experience, etc.

6. Stay involved. Even if you hire someone to write or produce your newsletter, you need to stay involved. No one knows better than you what kinds of information your customers want and need.

7. Evaluate your efforts. Does it bring in new business, boost sales to current customers, or give your sales people a foot in the door?

Sales Promotion

Sales promotions are marketing activities that don't fit into the other categories. They stimulate consumer purchases and dealer effectiveness in the short run. At the same time, they may decrease profits during the short run. Figure 4.1 on p. 208 illustrates how sales promotions produce a temporary kink in the sales curve, and not necessarily a long-term increase in sales.

Sales Promotional ideas include:

Price reduction	Sampling
Trial size	Premium in or on package
Refunds	Sweepstakes or games
Trade shows	Laundromat and grocery store bulletin boards
Sandwich boards	Truck sides and ends
Telephone recordings	Business cards
Signs	Sponsorships
Community activities	Coupons
Free on customer's birthday	

Figure 4.1: Effect of Sales Promotions on Sales and Profits

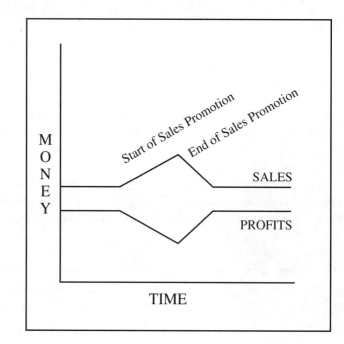

Advertising

Advertising is a nonpersonal sales presentation usually directed to a large number of potential customers (your target market):

- usually involves mass media such as newspapers, television, radio, magazines, and billboards

- paid for by individual or organization who is in some way identified in the message

- seeks to achieve communication goals rather than direct sales objectives

- improves the likelihood that the customer will come to the store, or buy the product or service

- to have real impact, you need to run an ad several times, but at a cost of about $350 per ad, you may not be able to afford running on a regular basis

A heavier emphasis is placed on advertising when:

- the target market is a mass market

- the product or service is purchased frequently

- competition from similar products/services is high

- the goal is to create awareness of a new product/service

- marketing strategy is to introduce the product quickly

- your market already perceives a need for the product category, but you need to distinguish yourself from the competition

Table 4.1 reveals the benefits and the shortfalls of various advertising media. You may find it helpful to review this table as you select promotional tools for your business.

Table 4.1: Advantages and Disadvantages of Advertising Media

Advantages	Disadvantages
Newspapers	
• short lead time	• low readership under 18
• distribution of message to your geographic territory	• read in a hurry
• size and shape flexibility	• overcrowded Wed - Fri
• catalogs for in-house buying	• low selectivity
• broad consumer acceptance and use	• small "pass along" audience
• free help often available to create and produce ad	• low quality production
	• a price oriented medium - most ads are for sales
Magazines	
• high selectivity	• wasted circulation
• receptivity of magazine audience	• long lead time
• economy of reaching a mass market	• high space and creative costs
• psychology of attention	
• repeat exposure	
• high quality production	
• smaller page permits even small ads to stand out	
Television	
• combination of sight & sound	• negative evaluation
• approximates face-to-face	• nonselectivity
• contact mass audience coverage	• fleeting impression
• many viewers watch commercials	• less commercial watching—remote controls and VCRs
• low cost per exposure	• clutter
• credibility-builder	• high cost for creative and production
	• limited amount of information can be communicated

Table 4.1: The Advantages and Disadvantages of Advertising Media *(cont.)*

Advantages	Disadvantages

Radio

Advantages	Disadvantages
• personal medium	• no demonstrations
• universal medium - people listen anywhere	• fleeting impression
• can target your market	• chaotic buying
• selectivity	• hard to get high reach
• speed & flexibility	• clutter
• low cost	• need to get immediate attention
• favorable psychological effect	
• free creative help is usually available	
• rates can generally be negotiated	

Direct Mail

Advantages	Disadvantages
• most personal & selective	• long lead time for creative printing and mailing
• minimum of waste circulation	• costly in terms of prospects reached
• copy can be extremely flexible	• junk mail image
• message can be as long as necessary	• getting and maintaining good mailing lists
• your message is hidden from your competition until it's too late for them to react	

Outdoor

Advantages	Disadvantages
• highly flexible	• widely used consumer good or much wasted circulation
• low cost/contact	• national campaign cost high
• excellent for reminder ads	• no lengthy copy

Yellow Pages

Advantages	Disadvantages
• reach ready prospects	• competition is listed
• reasonably inexpensive	• creativity difficult
• long life	

Specialty Ads

Advantages	Disadvantages
• reminder for current customers	• not good for getting new customers
• attention grabbers	

Evaluating Your Promotional Tools

Different promotional tools and media have different abilities to reach your target audience and to communicate effectively. When comparing different media or promotional tools, be sure to compare apples to apples by using the following factors.

Cost Per Thousand: the cost to reach 1,000 people with your message through a particular medium, calculated by dividing the ad or commercial cost by the circulation, viewership, or listenership counts.

Waste: the percentage of the audience of an advertising medium that is not part of your target market.

Target Cost Per Thousand: the cost to reach 1000 people in your target market with your message through a particular medium.

Return Rate: in direct mail or telemarketing, measures the number of orders per 100 contacts.

Promotional Cost per Inquiry: total promotional dollars divided by the number of inquiries.

Promotional Cost per Order: total promotional dollars divided by the number of orders the promotion encouraged.

Trade Winds Grocery, Jerry Lee: Jerry Lee determined that the direct mail proposal for his market would cost approximately $1,000. There are 5,900 people in his target area. His target audience is 4,100 people. Jerry Lee evaluated his proposal as follows:

Cost per Thousand
$1,000 ÷ 5,900 = $.16949
$.16949 x 1,000 = $169.49

Waste
5,900 - 4,100 = 1,800
1,800 ÷ 5,900 = 31%

Target Cost per Thousand
$1,000 ÷ 4.1 = $243.90

Return Rate
As determined by Direct Mail Marketing Data = 4%

Promotional Costs per Inquiry

If Jerry Lee's Promotion has an inquiry rate of 6 percent of the 4,100 people in his target area, his target audience would generate 246 inquiries. With a $1,000 budget, this would mean that each inquiry would cost him $4.07.

Promotional Cost per Order

If Jerry Lee's store generated 4 percent in sales (164 sales) with a total cost of $1,000, promotional costs per order would be $6.10.

Jerry Lee chose direct mail as one of his promotional tools because it offered good exposure to his target audience with a low cost per order.

You will find it extremely valuable to evaluate your promotional tools, as Jerry Lee did, before making a selection. The cost-benefit analysis will guide you in your decision-making process.

You Have Completed Challenge 4

By completing this section, you have discovered that the effectiveness with which you gather information and the quality of the information gathered often makes the difference between a successful and unsuccessful promotion. You have learned what information needs to be gathered and how to use that information as the foundation for your promotion plan. With this solid foundation, you will be able to create promotions that will be effective and obtain a synergy from your promotions.

You Leave Challenge 4 with the Following:

Information: You have gained the skill to objectively evaluate promotional ideas. You have learned how to translate the features of your product or service into a benefit that your customers will buy. You understand how to position your product or service to differentiate yourself from your competition. And you have learned how to select the most cost effective promotional tool to achieve your communication goal.

Tools: The workshops you completed can be used as tools to develop your plan for communicating with your market. You can use the workshops to determine the purpose of each promotion, to uncover your customers "hot buttons," to see how you compare with your competition, and to evaluate your promotions. In addition, the copywriting tips and list of words can be used to help you get started writing your copy. Finally, the descriptions of promotional tools can be used to generate more effective means of communicating with your market.

Learning: In this Challenge, you have learned that your customers don't buy what you sell, they buy the benefit your product or service provides. You have also learned that each customer group may have a different benefit as its "hot button." You have also discovered a wide variety of promotional tools that you may have been overlooking in your past promotional efforts.

Networking: By using the information you have learned in this Challenge, you will be better able to utilize your current promotional resources, whether that be the media reps, a freelance copywriter or graphic artist, or an advertising agency. From another point, you have discovered suggestions for developing a network by following some of the word-of-mouth marketing ideas.

Challenge 4 Self Assessment

To check your understanding and to get you started developing your promotional message and selecting your promotional strategies, answer the following questions.

Pages 159 - 212

( ) I can list two specific promotional goals that I would like to achieve in the next year.

( ) I can list the features and benefits of my product or service.

( ) I am able to determine which benefits are most important to each market niche I plan to serve.

( ) I can describe the picture I would like to paint in my customer's mind in one to three sentences.

( ) I can list the information I need to provide prospects to encourage them to call and request more information.

( ) I can list the information I need to provide to prospects to motivate them to call and place an order.

( ) I am able to list three strategies that I might implement to encourage more referrals to my business.

( ) I can define the steps I need to take to assure that I am sending direct mail and not junk mail.

( ) I can list three changes I will make to improve my sales presentations.

( ) I can describe three ways to use the telephone in my marketing efforts.

( ) I can list two public relations strategies that I will consider implementing.

( ) I am able to explain how sales promotions effect both sales and profits.

( ) I can describe when advertising is a cost effective promotional tool.

Take Another Look

RECORD ANYTHING FROM YOUR CHALLENGES, YOUR PERSONAL WORKSHOPS, OR YOUR PERSONAL REFLECTIONS THAT YOU WANT TO REMEMBER.

Review the results of your Challenge 4 Self-Assessment. Which areas do you still need to work on? Follow up on these areas by reviewing appropriate sections of the Challenge.

You Have Mastered

Marketing Concepts

In exploring small business marketing, you discovered that every activity conducted by your business influences your marketing. Marketing is not just a couple of activities that you periodically undertake. It is the entire mindset of your business, from the quality of your product or service, to the level of customer service, to the way goods or services are delivered to your customers. Marketing begins before you open your doors, and continues nonstop until you close your business.

You found that marketing for small business is different than for your larger competitors. Limited funds and staff require you to market smarter than competitors who can outspend you. Doing a little of what your competitors do is seldom effective. So you have to develop different marketing strategies.

As you have learned, the key to marketing smarter is to focus. Focus on the markets most likely to be your customers. Focus on the products or services most likely to satisfy their needs better than your competitors. Focus on the hundreds of little details that your larger competitor overlooks. To focus, begin by thinking like a customer. Compile information about the markets you can serve and their needs. Look at what your competition is doing, and at your strengths and weaknesses. Then prioritize your markets, and their needs. Set specific objectives. Once you know where you want to go, it becomes much easier to get there.

By completing the marketing Challenges, you have developed a marketing plan. But that plan is not set in stone. Be flexible enough to change it as your customers change. Experiment with different marketing strategies. Regularly review your progress so you can do more of what works and eliminate the marketing strategies that don't help you achieve your goals.

Once you have selected your marketing strategies, develop an action plan to assist in the implementation of your plan. Monitor your progress monthly so you can reduce the number of fires you have to put out. The plan itself will get you nowhere; success is achieved by taking one step at a time. Make sure you don't miss that last step that may mean the difference between success and failure.

215

Now that you have implemented your marketing plan, review it to make sure you are doing the right things. Look at what your are doing right, and what you are doing wrong. But focus on whether you are doing the right things. Are your efforts adding value to your customers, or costs to your company?

You have learned how to collect the information you need for decision making. Make the marketing planning process easier by continually gathering information you need to make better marketing decisions. Then use the information you have gathered to fine tune your marketing plan, and make better use of your marketing dollar. Ask yourself every day, "What else could I be doing to serve my customers better or more efficiently?"

You have completed the challenge of how to best market a small business. Now you are ready to turn the plans that you have developed into action for your own business. It will be an exciting and rewarding time. Good luck!

Key Resources

Books

Upstart Publishing Company, a division of Dearborn Publishing Group, Chicago, IL. Call 800-235-8866 for a free catalog. List of titles include:

Launching New Ventures: An Entrepreneurial Approach, Kathleen Allen, 1995 Innovative entrepreneurship text that enables the students to plan and start a world-class venture guide that takes the reader from the first basic steps of developing an idea to creating a detailed business and marketing plan. Instructor's manual available. 496 pp., $35.00

Strategic Planning for the New and Small Business, Fred L. Fry and Charles R. Stoner, 1995. This highly practical text guides students through the strategic planning process using case histories and examples of actual businesses. Unique in that it is a strategy book aimed specifically for small businesses. Instructor's manual available. 256 pp., $24.95

Financial Essentials for Small Business Success, Joseph Tabet and Jeffrey Slater, 1994. This text stresses importance of common sense in overcoming the problems of poor record keeping and planning. Step-by-step guidance results in students learning to interpret financial reports and building the necessary financial tools for a profitable small business. Instructor's manual available. 272 pp., $22.95

Business Planning Guide, Seventh Edition, David H. Bangs, Jr., 1995. Designed for both beginning students and more experienced practitioners, this is a vital tool for putting together a complete and effective business plan and financing proposal. Contains three complete sample business plans. Available on CD-ROM. Instructor's manual available. 224 pp., $22.95

Anatomy of a Business Plan, Second Edition, Linda Pinson and Jerry Jinnett, 1996. The step by step approach assumes no prior knowledge of a business plan. This basic presentation enables the student or entrepreneur to prepare a start-up plan for a new small business or plan new strategies for an existing business. Instructor's manual available. 256 pp., $22.95

Market Planning Guide, Fourth Edition, David H. Bangs, Jr., 1995. Practical text that shows students how to create an effective marketing plan suited to the business' goals and resources. Features complete marketing plans for two actual businesses. Instructor's manual available. 257 pp., $22.95

Target Marketing, Linda Pinson and Jerry Jinnett, 1993. Text is a comprehensive guide to developing a marketing plan for your business. Broken into a simple three stage marketing process of research, reach and retain. Instructor's manual available. New edition Spring 1996. 176 pp., $22.95

The Start Up Guide, David H. Bangs, Jr., 1994. Walks students through every phase of small business start-up. Text is based on a hypothetical one-year process. 176 pp., $22.95

Steps to Small Business Start-Up, Linda Pinson and Jerry Jinnett, 1993. One step at a time, the student learns the mechanics of business start-ups and gets started on everything from record-keeping, marketing and business planning. Contains forms, examples and worksheets. Instructor's manual available. 255 pp., $22.95

Cash Flow Control Guide, David H. Bangs, Jr., 1990.Step by step guide to learning a cash flow control process for the small business. It uses a real-life example of a company that demonstrates how cash flow planning can smooth out some of the small business's roughest spots. 88 pp., $19.95

Keeping the Books, Second Edition, Linda Pinson and Jerry Jinnett, 1996. Hands-on introduction to small business bookkeeping, which may be used with students who have no financial or accounting background. It covers all the essentials and provides numerous sample forms and worksheets. Instructor's manual available. 208 pp., $22.95

Export Profits, Jack Wolf, 1993.Comprehensive guide that simplifies the complex subject of exporting. It assumes no prior knowledge of international trade and with the aid or resources, examples and sample documents covers all the aspects of exporting. 304 pp., $22.95

Cases in Small Business Management, John de Young, 1994. More than 50 intriguing and useful case studies focusing on typical problems faced by small business managers every day. Problem solving is encouraged through end-of-chapter questions that lead students through an analysis of possible solutions. Instructor's manual available. 288 pp., $24.95

Problems and Solutions in Small Business Management, Editors of Forum, 1995. A collection of case studies selected by the editors of the small business journal, Forum. A problem drawn from an actual business is presented and then followed by three possible solutions written by experts from a variety of areas within the field of small business management. 192 pp., $22.95

Small Business Source Book, Detroit, Michigan: Gale Research Co., 1995.

The Brass Tacks Entrepreneur, by Jim Schell. New York: Henry Holt and Company, Inc. 1993.

Magazines

Black Enterprise, 130 5th Avenue, 10th Floor, New York, NY 10011-4399. (212) 242-8000.

D&B Reports, 299 Park Avenue, New York, NY 10171. (212) 593-6724.

Entrepreneur Magazine, 2392 Morse Avenue, Irvine, CA 92714-6234.

In Business, J.G. Press, Inc., 419 State Street, Emmaus, PA 18049-0351. (215) 967-4135.

Inc. Magazine, Goldhirsch Group, 38 Commercial Wharf, Boston, MA 02110-3809. (617) 248-8000.

Small Business Forum, University of Wisconsin-Extension, Madison, WI 53706-1498. (608) 263-7843.

Associations

American Society of Independent Business, 777 Main Street, Suite 1600, Fort Worth, TX 76102. (817) 870-1880.

National Association for the Cottage Industry, Box 14850, Chicago, IL 60614-0850. (312) 472-8116.

National Association for the Self-Employed, 2328 Gravel Road, Fort Worth, TX 76118. (800) 232-6273.

National Small Business Association, 1155 15th Street NW, Washington, DC 20005-2706. (202) 293-8830.

On-Line Services

America Online: (AOL). Call 800-827-6364 for a free trial membership.

CompuServe: Call 800-487-0588 for a free trial membership.

Prodigy: Call 1-800-PRODIGY ext. 358 for a free trial membership.

Local

SBDC: Contact you local Small Business Development Center for local publications.

Library

Check with your librarian for resource recommendations.

Key Word Glossary

Benefit: Anything deriving from a product/service that will be an advantage to the customer.

Brand: A name, term, sign, symbol, design or some combination used to help customers recognize and differentiate products/services.

Breakeven: The point in business where revenue from sales equals business expenses. Money made beyond this point is profit.

Competitive edge: The way in which a business satisfies a customers' needs better than competitors do.

Concentrated target market: Selecting one or two groups as the target market.

Demographics: The statistical study of human populations, especially with reference to size and density, distribution and vital statistics.

Feature: The characteristics of a product or service that tells what the product does, how it works, or what services it provides.

Fixed costs: Regular costs of business which do not change regardless of the number of customers.

Generic product: A product or service that is not branded.

Market potential: The total annual sales of a producer or service by all businesses providing that product or service to a specific segment of the market.

Market segmentation: Defining your potential customers by various characteristics such as demographics, purchasing habits, or life styles.

Mass market approach: Using the same pricing, promotional, and place strategies to reach *all* customers.

Multiple target markets: Using different marketing strategies to reach different market subgroups based on demographic, geographic, and psychographic usage rates and/or customer behaviors.

Niche: A targeted market segment that you determine is not adequately being served by the current competition.

Psychographics: The study of the psychological profiles of individuals that is used to segment markets.

Qualitative research: Research which usually involves small groups of people in an informal, unstructured setting. A focus group is a type of qualitative research.

Quantitative research: Research which usually involves asking structured questions to large groups of people. A telephone survey is an example of this type of research.

Sample: The group of respondents that an interviewer surveys.

Target market: A group of potential customers with similar needs which can be identified by a company.

Trademark: A legally recognized name, word, or symbol used to identify a product or service.

Variable cost: Expenses that fluctuate based on the amount of sales.

Warranty: A guarantee that a business will replace a product or refund part or all of the purchase price if the buyer finds it to be defective or lacking in some way.

Personal Workshops for Your Use

Your participation in Personal Workshops is a key factor in the success of your mastery learning experience. These workshops provide you with the opportunity to react and to respond to the information given in each lesson. As you complete each workshop, you are encouraged to apply your knowledge to your own business experience.

The Personal Workshops presented in this guide are reprinted on the following pages. While the directions needed to complete each exercise are included on each workshop page, the information necessary to prepare you for the activity is not. To fully understand each Personal Workshop, you will need to read the text and the Personal Workshop Preparations that precede each exercise.

Personal Workshop #1
Thinking Like the Customer

Imagine that you are the customer and that you are skeptical about parting with your money for the product or service your company offers. Determine from your answers how well you convince yourself that your company satisfies your needs.

1. What are the three most important things you want me to know about your product or service?

    #1:

    #2:

    #3:

2. Why are they important to me?

    #1:

    #2:

    #3:

3. How does your product/service excel when compared with others offering it?

    #1:

    #2:

    #3:

4. How do you feel your company is better and different from my current supplier?

5. Why should I believe that you know what you are doing?

6. How do you make it more convenient for me to buy than does my current supplier?

7. How does your pricing compare with my current supplier?

THE PURPOSE OF THIS WORKSHOP IS TO EVALUATE HOW MUCH TIME AND MONEY YOU ARE NOW INVESTING IN YOUR MARKETING; TO DETERMINE WHAT YOUR MESSAGE IS; AND WHAT STEPS YOU TAKE TO BE CONSISTENT IN COMMUNICATING YOUR MESSAGE.

Personal Workshop #2
How We Market Now

1. In the past year, how many dollars did you invest in marketing?

$

2. For comparison, how many dollars did you spend in the past year on your business vehicle?

$

3. List below, by month, any major market research or promotional activity you completed in the past year:

January

February

March

April

May

June

July

August

September

October

November

December

4. I am a stranger and I ask you what your marketing message is. What would you say?

5. Do you approach your sales promotion literature with a single theme?

   Yes (   ) No (   )

6. If Yes, what is your theme?

7. Do you utilize consistent design, color, paper, etc. to tie together your materials?

   Yes (   )   No (   )

8. Are all employees trained to give the same, basic marketing story about your business?

   Yes (   )   No (   )

Personal Workshop #3
Is Your Business Market Driven?

1. Do you conduct research on customer needs before you design a new product or service?

   Yes ( )   No ( )

1a. If No, why not?

2. Can you directly relate your product or service features to documented customer needs?

   Yes ( )   No ( )   If Yes, pick one product for Questions 2a-2c.

2a. Which product/service ?

2b. Which feature?

2c. Which need?

3. How often do you survey the satisfaction of your customers?

3a. How do you do this?

4. Do you routinely ask for customer suggestions?

   Yes ( )   No ( )

5. If Yes, how do you do this?

6. Do you maintain detailed records on customer background, needs, past comments?

   Yes ( )   No ( )

7. Do you train all employees in selling new products or services?

   Yes ( )   No ( )

8. Have you given your employees a written policy on handling customer complaints and requests for return?

   Yes ( )   No ( )

9. If Yes, do you use customer complaints to improve your product or service?

   Yes ( )   No ( )

THE PURPOSE OF THIS WORKSHOP IS TO FOCUS ON HOW WELL YOU CURRENTLY MIX THE THREE TYPES OF CUSTOMERS PRESENTED ABOVE. IT PROVIDES GUIDANCE IN ADJUSTING YOUR MARKETING EFFORTS TO BETTER ACHIEVE THE BALANCE BETWEEN CUSTOMER SATISFACTION AND PROFITABILITY.

Personal Workshop #4
Our Current Customer Family

1. What percentage of your customers account for 80% of your sales?

_____%

1a. List the names of your key customers (or attach a computer printout):

2. On average, how many times did the typical customer in this group buy from you last year?

3. How could you go about getting just one more order per year from each of them?

4. What new skills, techniques or technology did you learn about in the past year from your customers?

5. Which specific customers provided this new knowledge?

6. How do you go about finding the "knowledge rich" customer?

7. When you want to know the latest in your business, which customers do you call?

8. What methods for staying in touch with business leaders do you find most convenient? (Personal contact, newsletters, on-line, etc.)

9. What communication methods have you been wanting to try?

Personal Workshop #5
What's My Problem?

Marketing Problem #1:

Marketing Problem #2:

Information Needed— Problem #1:

Information Needed—Problem #2:

Personal Workshop #6
Assessing The Environment

Economic

What is going to happen to the economy over the next six months? Next year?

How will this impact your business?

Political/Legal

What laws do you currently have to comply with?

What changes are likely to occur in legislation that affects your business (i.e., pollution control, equal employment opportunity, product safety, advertising, price controls, etc.)?

Social/Psychological

What cultural trends will have an impact on the demand for your product or service?

What new trends can you capitalize on?

Demographic

What are the demographic trends (i.e., age, income, gender, ethnicity, family size, occupation, education, etc.) that may alter the composition of your customer base?

What is the likely impact of these changes on your business?

Technological

How will new technologies affect the need for your product/service?

How will new technologies affect the way your product/service is distributed?

How will new technologies affect the way your product/service is marketed?

How will new technologies affect the way your product/service is produced?

Environmental

What is the environmental impact of producing or distributing your product?

THE PURPOSE OF THIS WORKSHOP IS TO DEFINE THE DIFFERENT NICHES THAT YOU SERVE; TO BEGIN TO PRIORITIZE THE NICHES THAT YOU COULD SERVE; TO GIVE YOU AN IDEA OF HOW DIFFERENT YOUR MARKETS MAY BE.

Personal Workshop #7
Consumer Markets

	Market A	Market B	Market C
Age			
Sex			
Family Life Cycle			
Income			
Occupation			
Education			
Location			
Market Size from Census Data			

THE PURPOSE OF THIS WORKSHOP IS TO DEFINE THE DIFFERENT NICHES THAT YOU SERVE; TO BEGIN TO PRIORITIZE THE NICHES THAT YOU COULD SERVE; TO GIVE YOU AN IDEA OF HOW DIFFERENT YOUR MARKETS MAY BE.

Marketing Workshop #8
Business/Industrial Markets

	Market A	Market B	Market C
SIC			
Number of Employees			
Geographic Location			
Carry Ethnic Products			
Part of a National Chain			
Decision Maker			
Gatekeeper			
Size of Market from County Business Patterns			

THE PURPOSE OF THIS WORKSHOP IS TO GAIN AN UNDERSTANDING OF HOW DIFFERENT NICHES DIFFER; TO DETERMINE WHAT IS MOST IMPORTANT TO EACH MARKET SEGMENT; TO PROVIDE IDEAS FOR PRODUCT OR SERVICE IMPROVEMENTS; TO PROVIDE IDEAS FOR PROMOTIONAL MESSAGES.

Personal Workshop #9
Understanding My Customers' Needs

	Market A	Market B	Market C
How do your customers perceive your products/services?			
What do they want from a business like yours?			
What goods or services should you be marketing?			
What can you do to make it easy for people to buy from you?			

THE PURPOSE OF THIS WORKSHOP IS TO QUALIFY THE SIZE OF EACH MARKET NICHE; TO ESTIMATE THE POTENTIAL OF EACH MARKET NICHE; TO PROVIDE A POTENTIAL FUNDER WITH OBJECTIVE PROOF THAT YOU HAVE A VIABLE BUSINESS IDEA; TO DETERMINE WHETHER YOU CAN GENERATE THE REVENUE THAT YOU NEED TO BE SUCCESSFUL IN BUSINESS.

Personal Workshop #10
Estimating My Dollar Volume

Steps in Determining Demand Estimation	*Demand for Your Product or Service*
1. Define your target market	
2. Define the rate of consumption or usage	
3. Calculate the potential annual purchases in your target market (Multiply Step 1 times Step 2)	
4. Estimate your sales volume	
5. Determine your selling price	
6. Project your dollar volume (Take the result of Step 4 x Step 5)	

THE PURPOSE OF THIS WORKSHOP IS TO GAIN AN UNDERSTANDING OF YOUR COMPETITORS' STRENGTHS AND WEAKNESSES; TO PROVIDE A FRAMEWORK TO MEASURE YOUR BUSINESS AGAINST YOUR COMPETITION; TO PROVIDE INSIGHT INTO THE MOST LUCRATIVE STRATEGIES FOR YOUR BUSINESS; TO PROVIDE INFORMATION NEEDED TO DIFFERENTIATE YOURSELF FROM YOUR COMPETITION.

Personal Workshop #11
Assessing My Competition

	Competitor A	Competitor B
Years in Business		
Number of Employees		
Target Market		
Positioning		
Strengths		
Weaknesses		
Technical Abilities		
Customer Service		

THE PURPOSE OF THIS WORKSHOP IS TO UNCOVER YOUR STRENGTHS AND WEAKNESSES; TO LOOK AT YOUR BUSINESS FROM YOUR CUSTOM-ERS' POINT OF VIEW; TO DISCOVER POTENTIAL OPPORTUNITIES OR THREATS

Personal Workshop #12
SWOT Analysis

Strengths   *Weaknesses*

Opportunities   *Threats*

THE PURPOSE OF THIS WORKSHOP IS TO LOOK AT YOUR BUSINESS FROM YOUR CUSTOMERS' POINT OF VIEW; TO DETERMINE NECESSARY CHANGES IN POLICIES OR PROCEDURES IN ORDER TO BETTER SERVE YOUR CUSTOMERS; TO DIFFERENTIATE YOURSELF FROM YOUR COMPETITION.

Personal Workshop #13
A Look At My Business

1. What are your hours of operation? (include days of week and times of day)

2. What extra services do you provide? (special orders, parking, delivery, etc.)

3. What changes have you made in your business over the last two years? How have these changes impacted your business?

4. Has your customer base changed over the last two years? If so, how?

5. How important is location for your customers? How convenient is your location for your customers?

6. Describe the appearance of your business, inside and out.

7. What is your customer service policy?

8. From your customers' point of view, what might be a disincentive to buying from your business? (price, location, parking, selection, turnaround, etc.)

9. If your customers had to describe your company to a colleague in one or two sentences, what would you want them to say?

10. How do you promote your business?

11. What do your customers like about your business and its operations?

12. What would your customers change about your business and its operations if they could?

13. How do your customers view your employees? Would they hire them?

14. Why do your customers buy from you and not from your competition?

THE PURPOSE OF THIS WORKSHOP IS TO IDENTIFY THE FACTORS CRITICAL TO THE SUCCESS OF YOUR BUSINESS; TO PRIORITIZE THE IMPORTANCE OF EACH OF THESE FACTORS; TO RATE YOUR BUSINESS AND YOUR COMPETITORS ON EACH OF THESE FACTORS; TO DETERMINE WHAT YOU NEED TO CHANGE TO BRING YOUR BUSINESS UP TO PAR WITH YOUR COMPETITION; TO DETERMINE WHAT FACTORS YOU CAN CAPITALIZE ON TO GAIN NEW CUSTOMERS.

Personal Workshop #14
Critical Success Factors

A. Critical Success Factors	B. Weights or Importance (out of 100)	Your Business		Competitor A		Competitor B		Competitor C	
		C. Your Ratings	Score (B x C)	D. A's Ratings	Score (B x D)	E. B's Ratings	Score (B x E)	F. C's Ratings	Score (B x F)
Unique flavors									
Fresh									
Affordable prices									
Orders filled within 48 hours									
Consistent quality									
Preparation tips									
Totals									

THE PURPOSE OF THIS WORKSHOP IS TO LEARN TO WRITE SPECIFIC MEASURABLE OBJECTIVES; TO KEEP STRATEGIES OUT OF YOUR OBJECTIVES; TO DETERMINE WHERE YOU WANT THE BUSINESS TO GO.

Personal Workshop #15
Objective Writing

Target Market Segment	*Objective*	*Is it SMART?*

HE PURPOSE OF THIS WORKSHOP IS TO SET OBJECTIVES AND CHOOSE STRATEGIES WILL BRING ABOUT RESULTS; TO CREATE A HABIT OF ASSIGNING AND SETTING DEADLINES FOR EACH TASK; TO THINK THROUGH WHAT IT WILL TAKE TO IMPLEMENT A STRATEGY.

Personal Workshop #16
My Action Plan

Objective:

Strategy:

Activities to Carry Out Strategy	Person(s) Responsible	Start Date	Finish Date

THE PURPOSE OF THIS WORKSHOP IS TO DETERMINE HOW YOU WILL MONITOR YOUR PROGRESS FOR EACH OBJECTIVE; TO PLAN TO EVALUATE WHAT IS WORKING AND WHAT IS NOT WORKING; TO PROVIDE INFORMATION TO HELP FINE TUNE YOUR PLAN.

Personal Workshop #17
Monitoring My Objectives

List each of your objectives. Then explain how you will monitor the progress towards each objective. Each month, add the results to the results column.

Objective	How Monitored	Results

THE PURPOSE OF THIS WORKSHOP IS TO EVALUATE HOW WELL YOUR PRODUCT/SERVICE COMBINATION SATISFIES NEEDS EXPRESSED BY YOUR CUSTOMERS.

Personal Workshop #18
Our Product Assortment

1. For your two highest dollar sales products or services, indicate the key customer need you are attempting to satisfy and detail the features and benefits you have built to achieve this satisfaction.

Product #1:

Customer Need #1:

Product Features:

Product Benefits:

Product #2

Customer Need #2:

Product Features:

Product Benefits:

2. In what ways do you provide variety or breadth of choice for your product?

3. Describe one change in features and/or benefits you have implemented in the past year that was the direct result of a customer complaint or suggestion:

4. Describe one modification in product features and/or benefits you have implemented in the past year as the direct result of actions by your competition:

4a. How well received was this change?

4b. If not well received, why not ?

5. Describe how you believe your product features and benefits successfully exceed your customers' expectations:

THE PURPOSE OF THIS WORKSHOP IS TO EVALUATE THE CURRENT STAGE OF GROWTH OF MARKET DEMAND FOR YOUR PRODUCT OR SERVICE.

Personal Workshop #19
Where Are We in the Product Life Cycle?

Select one choice for each question below:

1. Our product features are:
   - ( )   Innovative and new
   - ( )   Copied by several competitors
   - ( )   Offered by broad competition
   - ( )   Not often found in the marketplace

2. Customer awareness of our product or service brand is:
   - ( )   Still small, but growing
   - ( )   Well established in "pockets" of the market
   - ( )   Widely known across the U.S
   - ( )   Has been declining

3. Our annual dollar sales growth for our main product line have been:
   - ( )   Growing in excess of 20% per year recently
   - ( )   Growing by 10-20% per year recently
   - ( )   Growing by less than 10% per year recently
   - ( )   Declining recently

4. In the past year, our profitability has been:
   - ( )   Greatly reduced by development costs
   - ( )   The best ever
   - ( )   Starting to level off
   - ( )   3eclining

5. We introduce new product designs and features:
   - ( )   At least twice per year
   - ( )   At least once every other year
   - ( )   Once in the past three years
   - ( )   Not in recent memory

Personal Workshop #20
How We Get Our Product to the Customer

1. Our products require:
   ( )   Extensive distribution
   ( )   Selective distribution
   ( )   Exclusive distribution

   1a. Explain your feelings for the above distribution strategy:

2. We:
   ( )   Sell directly to customers
   ( )   Use distributors and/or wholesalers to sell
   ( )   Use manufacturers sales representatives to sell

3. Physical location is important to our marketing strategy:
   Yes ( )   No ( )

   3a. If Yes, describe how you use physical location to draw attention to your business:

4. We have good availability of affordable, trained labor in and around our chosen location.
   Yes ( )   No ( )

   4a. If No, describe how you overcome this drawback to your location:

5. Close proximity to our suppliers is very important to our marketing strategy:
   Yes ( )   No ( )

   5a. If Yes, describe how you have arranged your location to facilitate transactions with your suppliers:

THE PURPOSE OF THIS WORKSHOP IS: TO ALLOW YOU TO DETERMINE YOUR PRICE FLOOR BY USING KNOWLEDGE OF YOUR FIXED AND VARIABLE COSTS AND BREAKEVEN ANALYSIS.

Six Step Personal Workshop # 21
STEP 1: How We Set Our Prices

Setting the Price Floor

1. Our total annual fixed costs are: $_____

2. Our total annual variable costs are: $_____

3. Our desired total dollar profit for the next year is: $_____

4. Our estimated annual unit volume of sales is:

    Product #1: $ _____

    Product #2: $ _____

    Product #3: $_____

Note: If your company sells a line of products or services, you may wish to calculate breakeven separately for each of the main product categories, therefore you will want to repeat this analysis several times.

5. Our variable cost per unit is:

    Product #1: $ _____

    Product #2: $ _____

    Product #3: $ _____

6. Our projected selling price per unit is:

    Product #1: $ _____

    Product #2: $ _____

    Product #3: $_____

7. Our profit contribution per unit is:

    Product #1: $ _____

    Product #2: $ _____

    Product #3: $ _____

8. Our breakeven in units is:

    Product #1: $_____

    Product #2: $ _____

    Product #3: $ _____

Note: If you wish to calculate separate breakeven points for several products, you will need to establish some method by which to assign a certain amount of your total fixed costs to each product. This is often done by determining the direct labor that goes into each product and using this percentage of total labor cost to break down the fixed expenses.

This Personal Workshop continues with Step 2

Six Step Personal Workshop #21
STEP 2: How We Set Our Prices

Setting the Price Ceiling

1. Do your customers consider your product or service:

( )   Fairly common

( )   Very unique

2. How aware are your customers of substitutes for your product:

( )   Not very aware

( )   Very aware

3. How easy is it for your customers to compare your product with competition:

( )   Not very easy

( )   Very easy

4. How significant is the dollar amount spent by your customers on your product or service as a proportion of their total expenditures in a year:

( )   Not very significant

( )   Very significant

5. How aware are your customers of the time and or money that can be saved by buying your product:

( )   Not very aware

( )   Very aware

6. How closely tied in your customers' minds is your price and their sense of quality:

( )   Not very closely tied

( )   Very closely tied

7. When examining your competitors, which of the following are true:

7a.

( ) You are one of a number of growing companies

( ) You are new in the marketplace

7b.

( ) You need to be known in the marketplace

( ) You are happy to be overlooked by competition

Note: If you largely checked the first boxes, you may be able to price slightly above your competition; if you checked the second boxes, you will most likely have to price below your competition until you become more well established.

This Personal Workshop continues with STEP 3

THE PURPOSE OF THIS WORKSHOP IS TO DESCRIBE WHAT FINANCIAL GOALS YOU WHICH TO ACHIEVE AND HOW YOUR PRICING WILL BE DESIGNED TO AID IN SUCCESS.

Six Step Personal Workshop #21
STEP 3: How We Set Our Prices

Setting Pricing Objectives

1. Have you recently made a large expenditure to develop or acquire a new product?
( ) Yes ( ) No

1a. If yes, what dollar amount of investment would you like to recover?

$ _____

1b. Over what time period do you hope to do this?

1c. What unit sales volume do you expect over this period?

1d. What selling price per unit must you charge to recover your investment?

$_____

2. Is one of your main marketing goals to gain market share quickly?
( ) Yes ( ) No

2a. If yes, what price level do you believe you must set, relative to competition, to attract significant interest among prospective customers?

$_____

3. Is your pricing an important part of your image marketing?
( ) Yes ( )No

3a. If yes, describe how you use pricing to substantiate your level of product quality:

4. Do your per unit costs drop significantly at some level of production?

( ) Yes ( )No

4a. If yes, what is that unit or dollar purchase volume level?

4b. How must you set your price to reach this level in the near future?

This Personal Workshop continues with STEP 4

THE PURPOSE OF THIS WORKSHOP IS TO SELECT ONE OR MORE PRICING STRATEGIES AND DESCRIBE THEIR IMPORTANCE IN YOUR OVERALL MARKETING STRATEGY.

Six Step Personal Workshop #21
STEP 4: How We Set Our Prices

Selecting a Pricing Policy

1. Is your desired product positioning to:

( )   Take advantage of the perceived superiority of your product

( )   Gain the maximum market share as quickly as possible

2. Based on your desired product positioning, designate which pricing policy is more suitable to your objectives:

( )   Price Skimming

( )   Penetration Pricing

3. Do you intend to have a single price or price list for your products, at all times?

( ) Yes   ( ) No

3a. If No, indicate how you will differentiate your pricing for different product/service combinations:

4. Is time of purchase an important factor in determining your pricing?

( )   Yes   ( ) No

5. If yes, how will you select your pricing to allow for different prices at different times?

6. Do you intend to establish "pricing families" for related products?

( ) Yes   ( )No

6a. If yes, describe how you will set this pricing:

7. Do you intend to offer different pricing for products individually and as a group?

( ) Yes   ( ) No

7a. If yes, describe how you will set pricing for product or service groupings:

8. Do you intend to use tie-ins or metering arrangements as part of your pricing?

( ) Yes   ( ) No

8a. If yes, describe how this pricing arrangement will be integrated into your marketing strategy:

This Personal Workshop continues with STEP 5

Six Step Personal Workshop #21
STEP 5: How We Set Our Prices

Choosing a Price Discount Plan

1. Which of the following will you use to set discounts:

( )   Total dollar sales of an individual order

( )   Total accumulated dollar sales over a period of time

( )   All dollar sales over a minimum amount

( )   For documented promotion using your product or service name

2. Do you offer a discount for paying quickly?

( )   Yes   ( ) No

2a. If yes, what is the percentage discount? _____ percent

And what is the payment time?: _____

3. Do you offer standard discounts to anyone who orders a specified dollar amount?

( )   Yes   ( ) No

3a. What is this discount?

4. Do you offer larger discounts once a new customer has ordered a certain number of times?

( )   Yes   ( ) No

4a. What are these discounts?

This Personal Workshop continues with STEP 6

Six Step Personal Workshop #21
STEP 6: How We Set Our Prices

Selecting a Geographic Pricing Policy

1. What is the traditional method in your industry of including freight costs in overall pricing?

( )   FOB Factory

( )   Freight Absorption

( )   Uniform Delivered Price

2. Are you able to modify your pricing in different parts of your distribution area?

( )   Yes   ( ) No

2a. If yes, describe how you do this:

3. Do you use zones in determining what freight cost to add to your pricing?

( ) Yes   ( ) No

3a. If yes, describe how you do this:

4. What different types of transportation do your customers demand?

5. How do you track the costs of these various methods?

6. How do you use this costing information to negotiate better rates?

LAST YEAR, WHICH PROMOTIONAL GOAL IT HELPED TO ACHIEVE. BE HONEST—ADVERTISING CAN NOT DIRECTLY SELL A PROFESSIONAL SERVICE.

Personal Workshop #22
Promotional Goals

Promotion	Generate Leads	Qualify Leads	Reinforce Selling	Create Awareness	Directly Sell

Consider eliminating or modifying any promotions that only created awareness. Check off the promotions you need to reconsider. By consciously thinking about the purpose of your promotions, you will be better able to objectively decide which promotions work for you and which do not. This will allow you to modify promotions to make them work harder or eliminate them altogether.

Personal Workshop #23
Features vs. Benefits

1. List the features (characteristics) of your product or service.

2. For each feature, list how the customer can benefit from that feature. Note there may be more than one benefit related to each feature. Benefits may differ by market niche.

3. For each market niche you plan to serve, prioritize the benefits you listed above.

Feature	Benefit to Customer	Niche A Priorities	Niche B Priorities	Niche C Priorities

THE PURPOSE OF THIS WORKSHOP IS: (1) TO COMPARE YOUR PRODUCT/SERVICE TO YOUR COMPETITION (2) DETERMINE WHAT IS IMPORTANT TO YOUR CUSTOMERS AND (3) DETERMINE WHAT YOU WILL COMMUNICATE TO EACH NICHE.

Personal Workshop #24
Describing Your Niche

1. Describe as completely as possible the main products or services that compete for your customer. For example, think not only of direct competitors such as another brand of potato chips, but also of other products that could satisfy a customer's desire to snack, such as pretzels, carrots, or popcorn.

2. Next to each of your major competitors, write a description of its strengths and weaknesses. Strengths could include the features of the product or service, or the benefits that are advertised. Weaknesses include missing features, or features that don't perform as well as yours do. (Look for ads or promotional material, or ask your customers what they think.) **Be sure to use a customer's point of view when you complete this section.**

Competitive Products/Services	Strengths	Weaknesses	Important Characteristics

3. Pick the two most important characteristics in the decision to purchase a product or service. Then graph where you and your competitors stand. **Be sure to do this from a customer's point of view.**

4. Once you have identified the niche or niches that you will fill, describe each niche in one sentence. For example, "The specialist in shoes of small size," or "The freshest produce of any supermarket," or "The restaurant with the most fun-loving waitresses."

THE PURPOSE OF THIS WORKSHOP IS TO WRITE A SENTENCE PROMOTING YOUR PRODUCT/SERVICE.

Personal Workshop #25
Writing Your Copy

The words I selected to use are:

My promotional copy:

Personal Workshop #26
Headlines

How would you answer the following questions about headlines you have used? As you answer, think about ways to modify the headline, or to create a new headline that would be more effective. If you don't have headlines that you have used, critique those of your competition.

Place your headline idea here:

Is the headline clear?

Does it communicate the benefit?

Does it speak to your most likely customers?

Is it interesting?

Can it be made more specific?

Does it work with the visual?

Personal Workshop #27
Checklist For Print Promotion

Answer each of the following questions as honestly as possible. Then edit your copy until you are satisfied with the answers to these questions.

Is it written as you speak?

How many points does it attempt to make?

How many products/services/promotions are emphasized?

Does the headline communicate your message?

Do you talk to a specific market or all markets?

Does the ad visually say what the wording says?

Did you BAF the reader: start with benefits, then advantages, then features?

Are you selling specifics, not generalities?

Could a competitor put his/her name on your ad and run it?

What could be eliminated to make it more effective?

Can you divide the copy up with subheads that sell?

Does the layout help draw the reader into the ad?

Does the copy help the promotion to do what you want it to: generate leads, sell the product, qualify leads, etc.?

Did you ask for the order or the inquiry?

Did you include your name, phone number and address on every piece in the package?

Place your edited ad copy here. Share your copy with your employees. What are their responses to the ad?

Index